The Swift Way to Learn Football

FOOTBALL FOR BEGINNERS: JOIN THE CRAZE AND LEARN TO LOVE IT, FOR SPECTATORS

LM TAYLOR

Contents

Introduction   vii

1. A BRIEF HISTORY OF FOOTBALL   1
   Origins and Evolution: From Rugby to
   Gridiron   1
   Milestones and Key Events in the
   Development of Football   3
   Cultural Impact and Growth of the Sport   8
   Notable Players and Legendary Teams in
   Football History   11

2. BASICS OF THE GAME   19
   Game Objective   19
   The Anatomy of the Field   22
   Playing Equipment   24
   The Football   28
   Game Structure   30
   Halftime and the Second Half   37
   Overtime   38
   Other Useful Tidbits   39

3. SKILLS ON THE FIELD   42
   Tackling Techniques   42
   Blocking Fundamentals   49
   Catching and Ball Handling   54

4. TEAM UNITS AND POSITIONS   60
   Team Composition: Offense, Defense, and
   Special Teams   60
   Roles and Responsibilities of Different
   Positions   65
   Positional Uniform Numbers   80

5. THE RULES OF FOOTBALL ... 82
Penalties and Infractions ... 83
Understanding Rule Enforcement ... 87
The Best Rule Changes in NFL History ... 88
Understanding the NFL Officials ... 92

6. PLAYS AND GAME STRATEGY ... 97
Common Offensive Formations ... 97
Common Defensive Formations ... 99
Special Team Plays ... 101
Offensive Strategies and Tactics ... 103
Defensive Strategies and Tactics ... 105
Game Management and Clock Control ... 107

7. YOUR GAME DAY GUIDE ... 112
Pregame Preparation: Getting Ready for Kickoff ... 112
The Procedure Before Kickoff ... 118
Player Pregame Rituals ... 119
Understanding the Broadcast ... 121
Key Statistics to Be Aware of ... 123

8. ICONIC PLAYS AND GAME-CHANGING MOMENTS ... 126
Unstoppable Plays ... 126
Game-Changing Moments ... 132

9. TEAMS, COLORS, AND MASCOTS ... 138
NFL Teams ... 138
NFL Team Colors ... 140
Team Mascots ... 142

Afterword ... 145
Glossary ... 149
Bibliography ... 153

Introduction

First things first – the term "football" in this book refers to what most of the world calls American football. For those who may not know, "football" outside of the United States is the sport that you probably know as soccer, or maybe even European football, if you live in America. But we are here to talk about football like Americans talk about football – think *Friday Night Lights*, *Rudy*, *The Blind Side*, *Any Given Sunday*, or one of my personal favorites, *Remember the Titans*.

Football can seem daunting when watching it for the first time, making new fans feel like outsiders while everyone around them is buzzing with excitement for their favorite team. At first, new fans might struggle to keep up with the game and feel left out of the banter shared by seasoned fans. You might also feel out of place, unable to join in the camaraderie that has become synonymous with football fans alike. Well, team, no need to worry because help has arrived with all the ins and outs you need to know to enjoy game day!

Football is one of the most-watched sports worldwide, with a staggering 1.7 million viewers watching in 2021 (University Living, 2023). Despite its incredibly impressive fan base, many fans are still left scratching their heads on the sidelines, unable to truly enjoy the sport or engage with its passionate fanbase. However, with this guide in hand, you, too, can join in on all the passion and pandemonium that comes with being a football fanatic!

Welcome, my fellow readers. I'll be your guide as we ride this football rollercoaster. I started off just as confuzzled as you. However, I loved the passion and camaraderie this sport brings to its fans, so I persevered, and let's just say I fell in love with the sport. Today, I can't get enough of football. I am a die-hard Pittsburgh Steelers fan who is ready every game day with my terrible towel (we'll cover this later) and I am decked out head to toe with Steelers colors (don't hold that against me, all you Chiefs fans). So, if you're ready to go from a newbie to a die-hard fan, I'm the gal to welcome you with open arms and lead you on a transformational journey from being a sideline spectator to a game-day guru.

You are in for one hell of a journey as we bridge the gap between confusion and confidence. We'll cover it all: the history and evolution of football, the fundamental concepts of the sport, how football became a beloved American pastime, the equipment needed, the intricacies of team composition, player roles and positions, and an overview of the rules governing gameplay to help you follow the action on the field. But that's not all, baby! We'll also cover a step-by-step game day guide with practical tips to make game day the highlight of your week. We'll cover team and player rituals, down to which players munch on chocolate chip cookies before a game, as well as iconic plays and game-changing moments that have shaped football into the sport it is today. Lastly, you'll have your very own cheat sheet of football terminology that will help you actively contribute to discussions with meaningful input. Gone will be the days when you feel like an alien in the football world; instead, you'll be ready for game day as you dive headfirst into the excitement and comradery of football fandom. I have included some fairly in-depth discussion on gameplay that you don't necessarily need to know in order to enjoy watching a game, but for those of you that want the nitty gritty – it's in here.

I'm sure you have noticed the sudden boom in football mania ever since Taylor Swift and Travis Kelce began their romance in 2023. It's no secret that their little love escapade has skyrocketed the NFL's popularity, attracting tons of new fans, particularly female and foreign fans. In addition, football has made considerable efforts to attract foreign fans by scheduling games abroad more regularly. For that reason, this guide couldn't have come at a better time. But don't think Swift became an avid fan overnight. When she first started dating Kelce, she was quite the noob to the sport. However, she was determined to become a fan and went as far as binge-watching Netflix to learn about the game (Gamble, 2024). If only she'd had a guide like this back then! Despite starting as a newbie, she quickly transformed into a super fan and has now become one of, if not the biggest, faces of football fandom.

So, my lovely readers, join me in saying goodbye to the days of sneakily Googling football terminology in the corner of the room, as this guide will cut through the complexity of the sport so you can feel empowered and excited to join the ranks of passionate football fans. The time is now to embrace the football hype and experience the thrill of watching and attending games with friends and family members. Alright, team altogether now, on three. One, two, three, GAME DAY!

CHAPTER 1

A Brief History of Football

The first official football game in history can be traced back to 1869, when Rutgers played Princeton (Hillyer, 2022), giving birth to America's all-time favorite sport, football!

ORIGINS AND EVOLUTION: FROM RUGBY TO GRIDIRON

Huddle up, because we're about to tackle the history of football. Football wasn't always touchdowns, bone-crunching sacks, and pinch-perfect passes. Nope, the roots of the sport back in its early days were more akin to soccer and rugby than the game we know today.

As mentioned earlier, the first official football match was between Rutgers and Princeton in 1869; however, the game was more like a hybrid of soccer and rugby than anything else. Nevertheless, this legendary match is what laid the foundation for the game we adore.

The rules were simple back then: Each team fielded 25 players, the field stretched for 150 yards, and the goalposts were only 10 feet tall. The objective was to simply kick the ball into the opposing team's territory and score a goal. But that's not all—hold on to your foam fingers because here's the real kicker: running with the ball, throwing the ball, and tackling or blocking players who didn't have the ball was an absolute no-no! The game back then was all about precision kicks and clever strategies. At halftime, teams would swap sides, and play would resume. For those of you dying to know who won the game between Rutgers and Princeton, it was Rutgers with a score of 6–4 (Richmond, 2023).

This first game resembled soccer more than anything else, but not long after football took a major shift from soccer-inspired rules to rugby-style rules. With this new evolution, football began to take shape into the game we know today. New rules more akin to rugby meant that the ball could now be picked up, carried across the field, and thrown, and tackles were permitted. These rules were implemented during the 1876 college football season. Despite the drastic changes in rules, the name "football" remained unchanged. However, as mentioned earlier since soccer is referred to as football in many countries, most English-speaking countries other than the USA use terms like "American football" and "gridiron" when referring to "football" (Hillyer, 2022).

Football was beginning to take shape; however, it was incredibly violent in the early years, and due to a lack of safety gear, there were tons of nasty injuries and even fatalities. This didn't sit well with the president at the time, Theodore Roosevelt. After 19 recorded deaths nationwide as a result of football,

Theodore Roosevelt threatened to abolish football altogether. Luckily, that wasn't the case, all thanks to 62 colleges in 1905 who gathered in New York to change the game and its rules. This meeting gave birth to the National Collegiate Athletic Association (NCAA). Among the colleges that met were Yale, Harvard, Princeton, and Columbia; however, many of the colleges still primarily played the game based on their interpretations (Burd, 2023).

MILESTONES AND KEY EVENTS IN THE DEVELOPMENT OF FOOTBALL

Over the years, there have been tons of alterations, additions, and jaw-dropping moments in football, but these have to be right up there with the most important developments throughout football's esteemed history!

1869–1880

- The first game of football was played between Rutgers and Princeton in 1869.
- Walter Camp was dubbed the "Father of Football" in 1880 as he shaped the game by introducing integral rules to the sport such as the downs system, the scoring scale, and the line of scrimmage, which laid the groundwork for modern-day football (Kuch, 2024).

1900s–1920s

- In 1920, football emerged as a professional sport as the American Professional Football Association (APFA) was founded, this would be known as the NFL (National Football League) in 1922.

- Superstars like Jim Thorpe and Red Grange, as well as legendary franchises such as the Canton Bulldogs, laid the groundwork for the NFL's eventual supremacy and spearheaded football's already growing fanbase.
- Other iconic football franchises, the Chicago Bears and the Green Bay Packers, were founded in the 1920s.

- This era also saw the rise of legendary stadiums being established, such as Lambeau Field (the Green Bay Packers home stadium) and Soldier Field (the home stadium of the Chicago Bears) (Kuch, 2024).

1930s–1940s

- The forward pass began to gain prominence in the 1930s. (A forward pass is when a quarterback throws the ball forward, meaning towards his team's goal line, to a teammate ahead of him to move the offense forward to gain yardage and even score a touchdown. The introduction of the forward pass brought increasingly inventive football strategies to the sport. Iconic coaches such as Paul Brown really made the forward pass shine by introducing more complex game plans to outwit opposing teams.
- World War II really disrupted professional football as more and more players were enlisted into the military.
- In the late 1940s, the NFL merged with its rival, the All-America Football Conference (AAFC) which helped further solidify the league's dominance over American sports (Kuch, 2024).

1950s–1960s

- The 1950s were a monumental era that saw the NFL's partnership with television; this was an enormous step forward for the sport.

- The success of this partnership was truly highlighted when the historic 1958 NFL Championship was broadcast nationwide. This game would forever be known as "The Greatest Game Ever Played" and forever revolutionized sports broadcasting in America.
- Jim Brown showcased his dominance as a football player in this era.
- In 1960, the AFL was established and quickly became a rival for the NFL. The AFL was the American Football League, which in the 1960s operated as an entirely different league and was an alternative for fans to watch as it promoted a more wide-open and high-scoring style of play. However, the rivalry between the AFL and the NFL didn't last long as the NFL merged with the AFL in 1967; thus, the first Super Bowl was born. Since that merger, the NFL has been divided into two conferences, the AFC (American Football Conference) and the NFC (National Football Conference). Each conference consists of 16 teams and operates as separate divisions within the NFL (Kuch, 2024).
- The Green Bay Packers were the team to beat when the Super Bowl first emerged.

1970s

- The 1970s were a golden era for the Pittsburgh Steelers and Dallas Cowboys.
- The Super Bowl had exploded and become a full-fledged cultural phenomenon in America. Halftime

shows and commercials became the norm due to the massive viewership.

- John Madden was a genius tactician, and he would later become the name brand behind EA Sports' popular football video game years later.
- The Pittsburgh Steelers achieved one of the most incredible winning streaks in sporting history. They would go on to earn eight straight playoff appearances, seven AFC Central division titles, and four AFC championships. Let's see those towels, Steeler fans!
- The Super Bowl became so popular it became an unofficial American holiday (Kuch, 2024).

1980s–1990s

- Football began to expand internationally. In the late 1980s, the first game abroad was played in London's iconic Wembley Stadium. These games abroad increased the popularity of football and brought along some new International fans.
- The San Francisco 49ers were the team to beat in the 1980s.
- The 1980s and 1990s were filled with talent, such as Jerry Rice, Joe Montana, and Lawrence Taylor, who defined this era of football (Kuch, 2024).

2000s–2010s

- The 2000s and 2010s were marked by technological improvements in the areas of tactical analysis and

player safety.
- Tom Brady and Peyton Manning defied this era with breathtaking displays as quarterbacks, while the New England Patriots were outstanding throughout these decades.
- Rule changes were enforced to ensure player safety due to the large number of player concussions (Kuch, 2024).

2020s:

- COVID-19 presented unprecedented challenges for the sport, including limited audiences, revised schedules, and intense testing protocols.
- Digital platforms transformed the experience; streaming games and virtual fan engagements became standard, showcasing the NFL's global sports dominance (Kuch, 2024).

CULTURAL IMPACT AND GROWTH OF THE SPORT

Football isn't just a sport in the United States—it's a way of life. Just think about it for a minute: from movies to video games, celebrities to Sunday traditions, football has sunk its teeth deep into the American consciousness. Think of those iconic films and TV shows growing up like *Remember the Titans, Rudy, "Friday Night Lights, The League, The Longest Yard,* and *Gridiron Gang,* and I could go on and on. We can't overlook the indelible mark that football has left on our screens and our hearts. These movies aren't just about football

—they are powerful narratives of perseverance, teamwork, and triumph over adversity. These movies capture the values inherent in football, resonating deeply with fans on a universal level.

Let's look at the Madden video game franchise. It's a smash hit, selling millions of copies year after year. These movies, TV series, and games not only entertain but also foster a sense of community among fans, creating a shared cultural experience that spans continents. But these massive media franchises and masterpieces are only the tip of the iceberg.

No discussion about football's cultural impact wouldn't be complete without mentioning the NFL's crown jewel—the Super Bowl. Year in and year out, this annual sporting extravaganza captivates countless fans and has evolved into a cultural phenomenon of unparalleled magnitude. Not only does it draw in millions of American fans, but fans abroad tune in every year to watch the Super Bowl as well. But remember, the cultural impact extends beyond the game itself; think of the star-studded performances that happen during the halftime show. Some of the world's biggest names have performed at the Super Bowl halftime show, captivating audiences worldwide with its grandeur and spectacle. I'm talking about the Rolling Stones, Bruce Springsteen, Madonna, Eminem, Justin Timberlake, Rihanna, and Beyonce—you don't get bigger names than that (McCarriston, 2024).

And while everybody loves a great show, the commercials at the Super Bowl are just as eagerly anticipated. All year round, countless people wish they could just skip a commercial; however, the Super Bowl is an exception. The commercials that air during the game have become an integral part of the experience, with advertisers vying for the attention of millions of viewers with innovative and memorable campaigns. Who can forget the Budweiser "Wassup!" campaign (Bhandari, 2023).

But here's the thing, while football lives to entertain the masses, its influence spreads beyond that. The sport has fused itself into the fabric of our society, even influencing how we get together and socialize. During football season, it monopolizes many Sundays in many households with the likes of tailgating before the big game, going to a sports bar, or inviting the entire squad to kick back and relax at someone's house with loads of snacks and refreshments as you watch the game. That's the true power of football—being able to bring us all together and foster a sense of camaraderie and community that makes football fandom so iconic. These Sundays are not only about football, but they are family traditions that have been passed down for generations to connect and spend quality time with the people we love.

Furthermore, football has almost become a common language that unites us from all walks of life, whether it's discussing the latest game or debating the success and qualities of different players and teams. Football provides a shared cultural bond that facilitates connections and fosters a sense of belonging, not to mention it's a great icebreaker. In addition, fantasy football has become a beloved pastime for countless fans. This platform allows fans to engage with the sport on a deeper level and fosters friendly competition among friends and colleagues. It is just another way to connect fans with fans and add another layer of excitement to the game by drafting the perfect team and managing your dream roster (Ki, 2023). I could write another entire book on just the topic of fantasy football, and plenty of them already exist, if you are interested in learning more.

Lastly, don't think football is only for us Americans; the sport is rapidly gaining more and more international attention and has spread its wings beyond American shores, captivating audiences in countries far and wide. The NFL's International Series, which features regular-season games played outside the United States, has helped to popularize the sport on a global scale. These international games have fostered the growth of fan bases in countries such as Mexico, Canada, the United Kingdom, and Germany. Football is a beautiful catalyst for connection that brings people from all walks of life together.

NOTABLE PLAYERS AND LEGENDARY TEAMS IN FOOTBALL HISTORY

Get your game face on, because it's time for a little trivia. Grab your shoulder pads because we're about to tackle some of the best facts, records, and achievements by notable players and iconic football franchises throughout football's rich history! This well help you feel more comfortable when those super-fans around you start talking about football's notable moments in history. And don't worry, the terms below are described in later chapters.

Team Facts

- The New England Patriots and Pittsburgh Steelers lead the pack for NFL titles, both boasting six Super

Bowls each under their belt. Hot on their heels are the San Francisco 49ers and the Dallas Cowboys, with five Super Bowls each. However, we shouldn't ignore the New York Giants, Green Bay Packers, and Kansas City Chiefs, as they each have four Super Bowls in their trophy cabinets (Schuller, 2024).

- Pittsburgh Steelers are the only team in the NFL whose head coach has won at least one championship since 1969 (Pistone, 2022).

- The New England Patriots came back from being down 28–3 in the third quarter only to win the Super Bowl in the fourth quarter. Thanks to a monumental display by Tom Brady and the rest of the team, the Patriots clinched their fifth Super Bowl victory, winning 34–28 on February 5, 2017. This would be known as the greatest comeback in NFL history (Pistone, 2022).

- Four out of five of the San Francisco Super Bowl wins happened in the 1980s. They were a truly unstoppable force back then and considered one of the best NFL teams in history, featuring Jerry Rice and Joe Montana on the same team.

- The Green Bay Packers won the first two Super Bowls (Pistone, 2022).

- The Miami Dolphins are the only team to have a "Perfect Season," winning every single game, including the Super Bowl in the 1972 NFL season. (Spajic, 2022b)

- The longest winning streak in NFL history is 23 consecutive wins by the Indianapolis Colts (Spajic, 2022b).

- The Pittsburgh Steelers have a 75% win rate at the Super Bowl, winning six out of eight times (Spajic, 2022b).
- Since the NFL was established, only 4 out of 32 active teams have failed to reach the Super Bowl, these teams include the Detroit Lions, Cleveland Browns, Jacksonville Jaguars, and Houston Texans (Spajic, 2022b).

Notable Players and Records

The NFL has some legendary players, but these guys arguably shine brighter than the pack.

Tom Brady

Tom Brady, also known as the GOAT (greatest of all time) is considered to be the best football player in history. He was the engine behind the New England Patriots utter dominance over the 2000s and 2010s and is the holder of countless records. Over his 21-year career, he has won seven Super Bowls and three MVP awards. He is a 3-time All-Pro and a 15-time Pro Bowler.

Here are five records Brady holds that are unlikely to be broken anytime soon:

- Record for the most touchdown passes to different receivers: 97
- Leading in combined career passing yards: 102,614
- Longest streak of consecutive seasons on a winning team: 21

- The oldest quarterback to win both AFC and NFC title games at 41 years old
- Most Super Bowl wins as a starting quarterback: 7 (Tallent, 2023)

Jerry Rice

Hall of Famer Jerry Rice was a true football player and is widely regarded as the greatest wide receiver in the NFL. He was a sight to behold and was adored for his precise route-running, impeccable hands, incredible work ethic, and unmatched ability to catch passes.

During Jerry Rice's 20-year playing career, he won three Super Bowls and was a 10-time All-Pro. This man was a machine and was the owner of 38 NFL career records by the time of his retirement.

He held the records in various categories:

- Career receptions: 1549
- Career receiving yards: 22,895
- Touchdown receptions: 197
- Yards from scrimmage: 23,540
- All-purpose yards: 23,546
- Combined rushing and receiving touchdowns: 207
- Total touchdowns: 208 (Raiders, 2024)

Lawrence Taylor

Arguably the best-ever New York Giants player, Lawrence Taylor, also commonly known as "LT," was known for revolutionizing the linebacker position. He was a force of nature on the field and was renowned for his explosive speed, exceptional agility, and ferocity as a pass rusher and run defender. Consistently making mince meat out of opposing offenses made him commonly considered one of the greatest defensive players in NFL history. He finished his highly impressive career with two Super Bowl wins, a Defensive Rookie of the Year award, three Defensive Player of the Year awards, and the 1986 MVP award.

Just have a look at these career stats:

- 132.5 quarterback sacks, excluding 9.5 sacks from 1981, as sacks weren't officially recorded until 1982
- Tackles: 1,088
- Forced fumbles: 33
- Fumble recoveries: 10 (Pro Football Hall of Fame, 2017)

Patrick Mahomes

Patrick Mahomes is considered one of the best players in the NFL, and the man is just getting started. When Tom Brady retired, somebody had to fill the shoes he left behind, and let me tell you, those shoes were mighty big! Yet, Patrick Mahomes has done an excellent job of being the star quarterback of the current era.

He has tons of records, but his most notable are

- Most yards gained in a single game: 734 yards
- Most plays in a single game: 100 plays, 88 passes, and 12 rushes

- Fastest player to reach 25,000 career passing yards in 83 games
- Fastest player to reach 200 passing touchdowns in 84 games

On top of that, he has won three Super Bowls, three MVP awards, and was named Offensive Player of the Year in 2018. (Pitman, 2024)

Travis Kelce

Another Kansas City Chiefs superstar and currently Taylor Swift's boo thang Travis Kelce is considered one of the best NFL players of all time. Travis has won three Super Bowls, is a four-time first-team All-Pro, and a nine-time Pro Bowler.

He also boasts NFL records for both the most consecutive seasons and the most overall seasons with 1,000 receiving yards as a tight end in a remarkable streak of seven seasons. He also holds the record for most 100+ reception seasons, with three seasons in total (Sportskeeda, 2024).

Joe Montana

Joe Montana, otherwise known as "Joe Cool," left one of the biggest marks in football history. His Hollywood-style persona and out-of-this-world performances made him the epitome of what every quarterback wished to be. He inspired countless young athletes; some could even say he was the original GOAT before Brady.

Joe Montana was inducted into the NFL Hall of Fame in 2000 and had a legendary career with the San Francisco 49ers with four Super Bowl titles, three Super Bowl MVP awards, and two regular-season MVP honors.

Joe Montana's legacy will never be forgotten. Montana ended his career with an impressive:

- Fourth in career passing yardage with 40,551 yards at retirement.
- Ranked fourth all-time in attempts with 5,391 attempts at retirement.
- Fourth in passing touchdowns with 273 passing touchdowns at retirement.
- Third all-time in completions with 3,409 completions at retirement.

The legacy Joe Montana left on the NFL will never be forgotten (Pro Football Hall of Fame, 2017b).

Peyton Manning

He was probably the only man who kept Tom Brady up at night. Peyton Manning was an unbelievable quarterback, and if it weren't for Tom Brady, he would surely have been the GOAT of the 2000s and 2010s. Manning's career is undeniably incredible. The man set the standard of what greatness looks like with achievements like 5,000 passing yards and 55 touchdowns in a single season. (Fadullon, 2022)

He won it all: two Super Bowls, five MVP awards, a Hall of Famer, and a hatful of accolades such as:

- The Most MVP awards: 5.
- Second most Pro Bowls: 14.

- Tied with the most 4000+ passing seasons: 14
- Seven touchdowns in one game
- 342.3 average passing yards per game in a single season in 2013
- The oldest quarterback to win a Super Bowl at 39
- The only player to lead two teams to win two Super Bowls with the Colts and Broncos
- Most football wins in NFL history: 200 wins (The Denver Post, 2023)

Peyton Manning was truly something to behold, and he was a wizard with the football.

I wish I could include all the superstars who have graced the field during the NFL's decorated history, but trust me, there are just too many! However, despite the immense talent the NFL produced these seven superstars surely shine amongst the greatest of them all.

Now that we know the history of football and just how monumental it is in American culture, let's learn about the basics of the sport by exploring its fundamentals.

CHAPTER 2

Basics of the Game

The NFL season is where magic happens for a total of 18 weeks. With a whopping 272 games in the regular season and an additional 13 games in the playoffs, it's a football fan's dream. Each game brings excitement, drama, and unforgettable moments on the football field.

GAME OBJECTIVE

Football may seem complex at first, but if we break it down, it really isn't too complicated. To start with, we have a rectangular field with a goalpost on each end of the field. Each team will have offensive players and a defensive players on this field; however, when one team's offense is on the field, the other team's defense is on the field, and vice versa. It is up to team playing offense to move the football downfield through precise passing and clever running plays to try and score points, while it is the job of the team playing defense to stop the opposing team in their tracks and limit them from running the show and scoring points. When one team's offensive turn is over, the other team's offense takes the field.

Now let's get to the main objective: Are you ready? Well, it's quite simple: The objective is to outscore your opponent—scoring is the name of the game. Scoring can include crossing into your opponent's end zone to score a touchdown while holding the ball, or a team can score by kicking the ball through the opposition goalposts for a field goal. While touchdowns are worth more points than field goals, every point matters in football, so don't sleep on the importance of field goals. The team with the highest score at the final whistle wins, and that's all she wrote.

Next, we have the downs system. This can be confusing for me fans. Essentially, this means a team has four chances, or "downs," to move the ball 10 yards forward (after they are initially tackled after kickoff or when the ball changes possession – more on this later). A "down" is when a player gets tackled and falls to the ground or their knees touch the ground. If a team makes it 10 yards before the four downs, then the downs will reset back to one, granting them another four chances to make 10 yards. Here's the kicker: If a team fails to make 10 yards after four downs, possession of the ball will change hands to the opposing team. Additionally, when a team is on their fourth down, they will have the option to either try to make up the yards to go for another first down or to kick the football. If they decide to kick, then they can either punt it downfield or attempt a field goal. This may sound confusing, but trust me, y'all will get the hang of it soon enough!

So, you may be asking yourself, *How long is a football game?* There are two answers. If you were to watch a football game, it would be approximately three hours long, including half-time, commercial breaks, and all that jazz. However, in reality, the actual playing time is only sixty minutes. You see, a game is broken down into four quarters, which are each fifteen minutes long.

In those 60 minutes of playing time, it is a full-on battle of strategy and skill, with eleven players from each team on the field at any given time. However, take note that offense, defense, and special players (we'll get to that later) will constantly be switching on and off the field, so it won't be the same eleven players all game long. Football is intense, fast-paced, and full of surprises, which constantly keeps us on the edge of our seats.

It doesn't matter if you're a die-hard fan or if you're just starting to get to know the sport; football is a spectacle of athleticism and strategy that has the power to captivate anybody!

THE ANATOMY OF THE FIELD

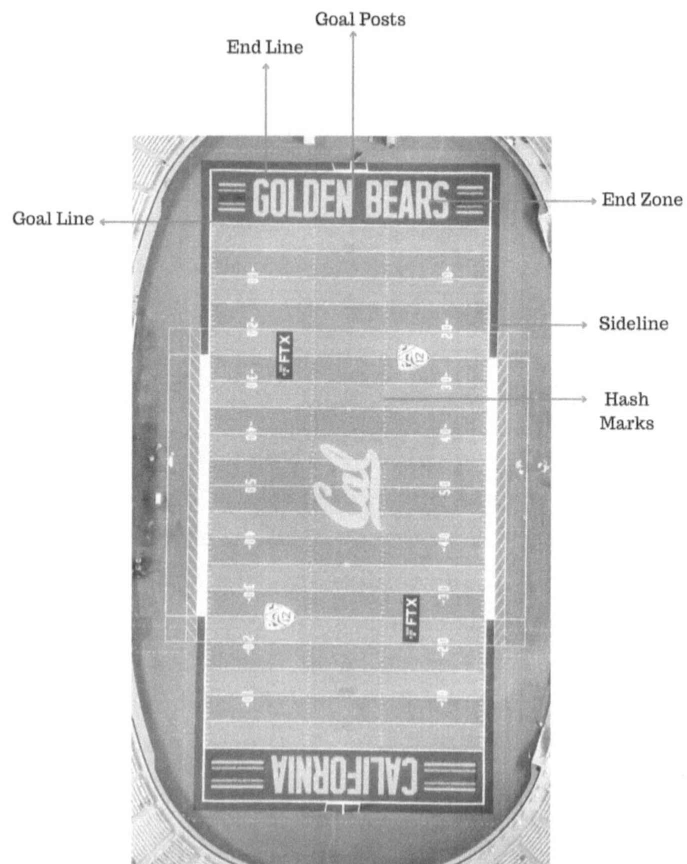

A football field is full of zones and markings, so it can be a little difficult to understand at first, but bear with me; after all, because of all these markings and zones, it got the nickname "gridiron" (Big Game USA, 2014).

A football field is a rectangular surface that is typically a grass field or an artificial turf that measures 120 yards in length and 53.3 yards in width. The field is divided into two end zones; this is where you score a touchdown. Each end zone is 10 yards deep from the goal line and stretches the entire width of the field.

Then we have the sidelines, which run the full length of the field on either side. They are 6 feet wide and 120 yards long, demarcating the playing area. A football field also has end lines that mark the boundaries of the end zones and measure 53.3 yards in length and 6 feet in width.

Goal lines are situated 10 yards from the end lines and this distance is what makes up the end zone. Yard lines are spaced every yard on the field and are used to determine a player's progress up the field. Lastly, we have hash marks. These are essential markings and consist of small sets of dashes situated in the center. They measure 24 inches in length by 4 inches in width. Hash marks are positioned between the 5-yard lines, running perpendicular to the sidelines. Essentially, hash marks help both the referees and the players pinpoint the precise placement of the ball during specific plays and aid in visually measuring distances. There are tons of markings on a football field, but every one of them plays an important role.

The line of scrimmage, while not a specific point on the field that can be identified in the above diagram, is a very important part of the game. The line of scrimmage is an imaginary line that represents the location on the field from which the offense is starting the first down. This is where you will see all the players line up at the start of a play. This line moves to a new location on the field when a player is tackled or goes out of bounds with the ball in their hands. For example, let's say the line of scrimmage starts at the 30 yard line on the first down of action. If a player runs the ball to the 35 yard line during the first down of play and is tackled, the starting point for the second down is the 35 yard line, which is now the new line of scrimmage. The line of scrimmage moves to wherever the player carrying the football is "downed", or goes out of bounds, or it may move if a team receives a penalty.

So, that is a summary of the field. But to simplify – the markings you care most about as a new spectator are:

- the goal lines – when a player either runs the ball through this line, or catches a pass on the end zone side of this line, he scores a touchdown.
- the yard lines – remember, the offensive players on the team need to move the ball toward their goal line at least ten yards within four downs or they lose the ball. Defensive players are trying to stop the offensive team from doing this.

PLAYING EQUIPMENT

A football player's gear isn't just the equipment they wear— it's their armor, their identity, and their means of survival on the gridiron battlefield! So, strap up your chinstrap because we're about to dive into essential football gear!

Helmet

Football can be a dangerous game, so safety is key. A player's helmet is their frontline defense from serious injuries and concussions. Many players also tend to rely on a mouth guard to protect their teeth from shattering or their tongues from unintentional bites.

Let's break down the helmet:

- **Chin strap:** This little strap is what keeps the helmet securely in place during the intensity of gameplay.
- **Air-filled interior pockets:** These pockets have saved many players from serious head injuries. They have pockets to provide comfort and cushioning and are designed specifically to mitigate the risk of concussions.
- **Face masks:** These are made from rounded metal material and must be in line with specific dimensions. They can't exceed 5/8 inch in diameter. Different positions often use different face masks; for instance, linemen often opt for cage-style face masks, as these provide greater protection against opposition contact. While quarterbacks and receivers tend to go for designs that optimize visibility, this also means their chins are more exposed.
- **Sunshades:** These aren't always necessary; however, some players incorporate sunshades into their helmets to protect their eyes from the sun's glare. Not only will this help maintain clear vision during the game, but it will also conceal their gaze from their opponents (Dummies, 2016).

Helmets are an essential piece of gear at all levels of football, and in a fast-paced sport like football, every advantage counts.

Jersey

A football jersey isn't just a piece of clothing—it's a badge of honor! It is a player's unique identity on the field and in our hearts as fans; furthermore, it marks a player's commitment to the franchise. Jerseys need to be a little bigger than a player's normal size if they bought a shirt at, say, Walmart, as a football jersey needs to be large enough to cover their shoulder pads.

Every NFL player who dons their team jersey gets a numeral to distinguish themselves from other players; this numeral will appear on both the front and back of the jersey. The numerals printed on the jersey are eight inches high and four inches wide.

Then, of course, a player's surname is printed on the back of the jersey in letters that are two and a half inches high and will appear on the upper back of the jersey above their given numeral.

Pads

If it weren't for protective pads, I don't even want to think about the number of injuries players would pick up. Pads are essential, as they absorb the intense physical impact players endure throughout a game, safeguarding their bodies from severe injuries. Football pads come in many forms, including thigh pads, elbow pads, hip pads, tail pads, knee pads, and, most iconic, shoulder pads.

Shoulder pads and football are synonymous with one another at this point, and for good reason. Shoulder pads stand out as one of the most important protective gear for a player as they shield a player's shoulders and sternum from harm. In addition, they also help protect their arms and rotator cuffs.

Some players, particularly quarterbacks, may utilize flak jackets to protect their rib cages and absorb the force of their intense throwing motions. Football pads, alongside the helmet, form a crucial line of defense, ensuring players can play the game with confidence and resilience.

Cleats

Cleats come in a variety of sizes, including 1/2-inch, 5/8-inch, 3/4-inch, and 1-inch lengths. Choosing the correct length of your football cleats is crucial for traction. For instance, if a football player is wearing the incorrect cleats on a muddy surface, they won't be able to bring their A-game. You may hear commentators discuss this during a game where it's raining, or if the field is grass versus and artificial surface referred to as "turf".

Choosing the correct cleats depends on several factors, including:

- **Conditions on the field:** Shorter cleats are generally worn on dry, firm fields, which makes a player less injury-prone. On a slippery grass field, players, especially big men like linemen, need to dig deep into the field to gain traction and would generally opt for 3/4-inch or 1-inch cleats.

- **Positions:** Preferred cleats can change based on a player's position; for instance, running backs and receivers tend to wear shoes that have fewer cleats compared to their larger, more physical teammates.
- **Field material:** When it comes to artificial surfaces, most football players will wear shoes that have dozens of rubber-nubbed 1/2-inch cleats on the sole of their shoes. Interestingly, some linemen prefer a basketball-type shoe when playing on artificial surfaces. The reason for these shorter and rubberized cleats is that on an artificial field, players want to glide over the surface; they don't want to have to stop and start every time they want to change directions, as this stop-start motion can take a toll on their ankles and knees (Dummies, 2016).

THE FOOTBALL

The old pig skin has become a symbol of American culture, although they aren't made of pigskin anymore; instead, they are made with cowhide. However, the name is still thrown around all the time.

We all know what a football looks like, but I bet you don't know the anatomy of a football. An American football is a leather ball that is shaped like a prolate spheroid for easy carrying. It is typically brown and features eight white laces where a player is meant to grip the ball.

Now let's get to the nitty-gritty stuff, like the dimensions of a football:

- Short diameter: 6.68"–6.76" (16.9–17.2 cm)
- Length: 11"–11.25" (28–29 cm)
- Circumference on the short axis: 21"–21.25" (53–54 cm)
- Circumference on the long axis: 28"–28.5" (71–72 cm)

A football's mass ranges from 14 to 15 oz (400 to 425 g), and it is inflated to a pressure of 12.5 to 13.5 psi (86.2 to 93.1 kPa). So, there we have it: America's most iconic ball (yes, I know it's technically not a ball) in all its glory.

GAME STRUCTURE

Gather up the team—it's time to huddle because it's game time. Let's get down to it and explore the ins and outs of how football is structured and what happens during game day, from the coin toss to kickoff, from offense to defense, from half-time to overtime. Let's get our game faces on!

The Coin Toss and Kickoff

Before the game even begins, the referee will hold a coin toss to decide how the game will begin. Both team captains will approach the referee, and the visiting team captain will either choose heads or tails as the ref flips the coin in the air.

The winning captain of the coin toss will decide one of the three options:

1. Which team will start with the ball?
2. Which direction will the teams score in?
3. The winning captain can defer to the second half - this means they want control of the football when the second half starts instead of at the start of the game.

The losing captain will then choose one of the remaining options that the winning captain didn't select. However, here's the catch: The losing captain will get the first choice of all three options in the second half if the winning captain does not choose to defer to the second half. You'd think something like a coin toss would be super straightforward, but not in the

NFL; it remains one of the most confusing aspects of football for newcomers.

Now that the coin toss is out of the way, it is time for the kickoff to signal the start of the game. During kickoff, the special teams (which will be covered in the following chapters) will take the field. The kicking team will transition to defense once the kick is made, while the receiving team will launch an offensive attack downfield as they attempt to make yardage toward the kicking team's end zone by avoiding tackles and staying in bounds. Following the kickoff, the offensive and defensive lines for both teams take their positions, setting the stage for intense gameplay.

There are a fair number of rules regarding the kickoff (this is one of those really detailed discussions of rules that you might not care about, but for those that do, read on!), including:

- The kickoff is taken at the kicking team's 35-yard line.
- All the kicking team players, except the kicker, need to stand with at least one foot on the returning team's 40-yard line before the kick.
- A minimum of nine returning team players need to be in the "setup zone" (between their 30-yard line and their 35-yard line).
- At least seven returning team players must have one foot on the "restraining line" (five yards from the kicking team's line).
- Up to two returning team players can stand in the "landing zone" (between their goal line and their 20-yard line).

- Only the kicker and the returners are allowed to move before the football is caught by a returner.
- If the kick lands or is caught in the landing zone, it needs to be returned.
- If the kick lands before the landing zone, it's considered a touchback, and the ball is placed at the returning team's 40-yard line. Normally, a touchback occurs when the ball enters the end zone and isn't brought back into the field of play. But in the case of kickoffs, if the ball drops short of the landing zone, it's also considered a touchback.
- If the football lands in the landing zone and then rolls into the end zone, the returning team must either return it or down it.
- If the returning team downs the football in their end zone after it rolls in from the landing zone, it's a touchback, and the football will be placed at the 20-yard line.
- If the football hits the end zone but stays inbounds, the returning team must return or down it. If downed, it's a touchback, and the football will be placed at the 30-yard line.
- Lastly, if the football goes through and out of the end zone, it will be considered a touchback, and the football will be placed at the 30-yard line.

Kickoff happens at various times during a football game. A kickoff will commence at the start of a game, at the beginning of the second half, after a touchdown or field goal, and at the start of overtime.

Offensive Play

The offense is where your point scorers shine and are the guys that march the ball forward, making yards for their team and scoring touchdowns. The offensive team is the one that has the ball. As mentioned earlier, they have four downs to move the ball 10 yards, and if they are successful, they can earn another four downs until they continue to make more ground up the field and eventually score a touchdown. Just remember, sometimes you only need one down to make those 10 yards. With clever play, smart running, and precision passing, you can make up to 30-plus yards on a team's first down.

The offense is made up of 11 players; these include:

- 1 x center
- 2 x tackle
- 2 x guards
- 1 x tight end
- 1 x tailback
- 1 x fullback
- 1 x quarterback
- 2 x wide receivers

We'll explore these positions in greater depth in Chapter 4.

Good offensive play is all about clever strategy, great teamwork, and being decisive when it matters to outsmart the opposing team's defense and put points on the board.

Scoring

Scoring is the most important aspect in football and when the clock runs out, whoever has a higher score wins. It's as simple as that. That being said, there are a variety of different ways to score in football, some worth more than others, but every point is extremely important so all methods of scoring should be considered.

Different ways to score points in a football game include:

- **Touchdowns:** This is the primary scoring method in football, and one fans can never get enough of it. A touchdown is worth six points and is when a player carries the football into the opposing end zone or catches a pass that has been thrown into the end zone.
- **Extra-point:** If a team scores a touchdown, they have a chance to add one extra point on the board by kicking the football through the opposition's goalposts from the two-yard line; this is also called a conversion.
- **Two-point conversion:** Instead of opting for the extra point, teams can choose to go for a two-point conversion following a touchdown by successfully crossing the goal line from the two-yard line on a running or passing play.
- **Field goal:** A field goal is a valuable method to rack up some points and are attempted as an alternative to trying to score a touchdown; they are worth three points and are achieved by kicking the football through the opposition's goalposts.

- **Safety:** These are rare points but very valuable; a safety awards the defensive team two points by tackling the offensive player in their end zone or forcing a penalty there. This is the opposite end zone that the offensive team is trying to reach to score a touchdown or field goal.

Defensive Play

The backbone of any great football team is their defense. Defensive play is essential to thwart the opposition from advancing the ball up the field to score points and to regain possession of the ball through strategy and skill. The primary job of the defensive line is to halt the offense from making 10 yards in four downs. This can be achieved by tackles, turnovers like fumbles or interceptions, and strategic play calling.

A down ends when:

- an opposing player is tackled and brought to the ground or their knees.
- a team scores points.
- a player running with the ball steps out of bounds.

- there is an incomplete pass thrown by the quarterback.
- there is a touchback.

For defensive players, there are two types of defense they primarily need to focus on: run defense and pass defense. Run defense is generally a collective effort between the defensive linemen and the linebackers. These guys will collaborate to keep a runner that is carrying the ball in check, with linemen engaging blockers and linebackers plugging gaps to thwart the advancing rushers. However, if a runner manages to evade both the linebackers and the defensive line, then it is up to the secondary defensive unit (safeties and cornerbacks) to make use of their speed to put an end to long runs or touchdowns.

Then there is pass defense, in which the coordination of every defensive player is key. Linemen will rush the quarterback to put pressure on their passing plays, while linebackers and secondary players will pull out all the stops to halt receivers and intercept passes. With intense pressure placed on the quarterback and skillful coverage of the receivers, there will be minimal opportunity for receivers to find open space. If a team can get both their running defense and passing defense on point, then the offensive team will have a tough day at the office.

Note that Chapter 4 contains more information, and a diagram, regarding the different positions of both the offensive and defensive players.

HALFTIME AND THE SECOND HALF

Halftime is a whirlwind of emotions and activity for players, coaches, and fans alike. For the players and coaches, they only have 13 minutes to regroup, re-strategize, and rehydrate. However, during major events such as the Super Bowl, halftime is generally a little longer. This is because more time is needed for the halftime show and awesome commercials to take place, but generally speaking, halftime is 13 minutes. In these brief 13 minutes, coaches may give pep talks, players refuel, and depending on the scoreboard and which side of it the team is on, tensions may rise and occasional clashes may erupt.

Despite only having 13 minutes, vital adjustments can be made, players can find their cool, and players emerge back on the field re-energized and filled with motivation. Halftime for players and coaches is an intense regrouping and reminds us as spectators of the intense pressure and focus required at every moment in professional football.

Luckily, for the fans, halftime isn't such a rollercoaster. As a fan halftime allows us the opportunity to stretch our legs, get a bite to eat, and go to the bathroom without missing any of the action of the game.

Once both teams have used the 13 minutes to the best of their abilities, both teams take to the field again in the third and fourth quarters. However, there are some instances when there is no winner by the end of the fourth quarter, as both teams end regular time in a stalemate – meaning the score is tied. If this is the case, overtime will be played.

OVERTIME

During the regular NFL season, games tied after regulation time will enter a 10-minute overtime period. There are only a brief 3 or so minutes between the end of regular time and the start of overtime for players to catch their breath. However, before the 10-minute overtime period begins, a coin toss will be made to decide which team starts with possession. In this overtime, both teams will have the chance to have possession (which means, then get a chance to score) unless the team with possession scores a touchdown on their opening drive. If that happens, the game is over. Additionally, each team gets three timeouts, and coaches can't challenge an official on instant replays in overtime as all reviews will be made by the replay official.

Once both teams have had possession and both fail to score a touchdown on their opening drives, the game will go to sudden death. If a game goes to sudden death, it means that the next team to score any points (touchdown, field goal, or safety) will win the game, but this must be done in the 10-minute overtime period. If, after the 10-minute overtime has been played, no team has scored any additional points, then the game will be declared a tie.

This is just for regular-season games; in the playoff season, no ties can occur. In the playoff season, overtime periods are 15 minutes long and are played until a winner is decided. Other than the fact that no team can tie in a playoff game, all the overtime rules remain the same for the playoff season. If after 15 minutes there is still no winner, another 15-minute over-time period will be played with a 2-minute interval between overtime periods. After the second overtime period, if the scores are still stuck in a deadlock the captain who lost the initial coin toss decides possession or which goal to defend unless the winner of the toss is deferred. If still tied after the fourth overtime, another coin toss occurs. Teams will play as many 15-minute overtimes as it takes until a winner is declared in a playoff game. It's important to note that there is only a 2-minute intermission between each period in overtime, but there is no half-time intermission after two overtime periods have been played. It just goes to show the stamina of these athletes.

For those of you wondering what the longest overtime game is in NFL history, it was a divisional playoff game between the Miami Dolphins and Kansas City Chiefs on Christmas Day, 1971, that lasted double overtime for 82 minutes and 40 seconds. The Miami Dolphins won that game 27–24. Double overtime games are incredibly rare and have only happened in six NFL playoff games, the most recent being an AFC Divisional game between the Baltimore Ravens and the Denver Broncos in 2012, which ended in a 38–35 victory for the Baltimore Ravens (FOX Sport, 2024).

OTHER USEFUL TIDBITS

If you've heard that Sundays are for football, then you'd be right! While some games are played on other days, the majority of NFL games are played on Sundays. This is because the NFL didn't want to compete with college football, which is generally played on Saturdays. Additionally, Saturdays used to be a work day for many people, so Sunday was the best day to draw in large crowds and it just stuck (CBS News, 2016).

Here's the thing: If you're a football fan, you're going to want to keep your Sundays open, especially from September until February, as these are the months the NFL season typically begins and ends. Throughout this period, each team will play in a 17-game regular season, which will be followed by a 14-team playoff series. In the playoff series, the championship game and Super Bowl will be played.

If you're wondering how the NFL structures this jam-packed schedule for each team, here's how:

- Six games against divisional rivals, meeting each team twice (once at home and once away).
- Four games against a division within its conference, which changes annually.
- Four games against a division from the opposing conference, also rotating every year.
- Two games against teams from the remaining divisions within its conference are determined by the previous season's division rankings.
- One game against a non-conference opponent from a division not on the regular schedule, determined by the previous season's division rankings.

But wait, there's more: teams will alternate between being the home team for nine regular season games and one preseason game or being the hosts for eight regular season games and two preseason games every year.

And if that wasn't enough football mania, the NFL further expands its reach internationally, with teams playing in global venues at least once every eight years. On top of that, four games from the regular season are scheduled to be played abroad. The countries these games are generally scheduled in include the UK, Germany, Australia, Canada, Mexico, Japan, Brazil, and Spain, due to the NFL's large fan base in these countries. The football season is truly a spectacle to behold!

Alright, now that we have the fundamentals down, it's time to uncover the skills football players need to execute on the field.

CHAPTER 3

Skills on the Field

Few aspects of football are more exciting than a bone-crunching tackle, and luckily for us fans, we get treated to a hat full of them every single game. NFL teams average between 37 and 47 tackles per game. We truly are spoiled when it comes to witnessing a great tackle in the NFL (StatMuse, 2024).

TACKLING TECHNIQUES

Tackling is one of football's cornerstones and an indispensable skill for a football player, especially as a defensive player. Tackling is when a player prevents another player from gaining yardage up the field by bringing them down to the ground, to their knees, or forcing a player out of bounds. Tackling is a defensive player's ultimate weapon to halt their opponents, put pressure on the offense, and regain their team's possession of the ball. Without solid tackling, a team may struggle to find their rhythm and take control of the game to secure victory. Skill at tackling is considered a fundamental element of the game, so much so that the expression "we've got to cover our blocking and tackling" is a common saying that is used even outside of the game of football to express the idea that, in whatever endeavor you take on, you have to master some basic skills in order to be successful. In football, if your team can't tackle, the other team will just continue to score more and more points and win by a wider and wider margin.

There are various methods players can use when tackling their opponents, depending on the game situation. Each method comes with its own unique technique. Take note that there are also tackling methods that don't sit well with the ref. These could result in a penalty for an offending player's team; for instance, a player leading with their helmet when making a tackle is a no-no and could cost their team serious yardage.

Generally, a player would lead with their shoulder and wrap their arms around the ball carrier when tackling; in most cases, this is the most effective and safest method to make a successful tackle. Furthermore, a tackle is only successful when an opposing player makes contact with a ball carrier and brings it to the ground; this action is called "down by contact." Essentially, this means that if a player trips or loses their footing and goes to the ground without any contact from an opposing player, then play will continue.

Every time a player makes a tackle, it will be recorded on a stat sheet. However, four types of tackles are recorded. These include:

- **Solo tackles:** These tackles are credited to a player when they are the only or primary player who made a successful tackle on an opposing offensive ball carrier. Only one player can be credited with a solo tackle in a single play. As far as stats go, solo tackles are incredibly important, as they highlight just how competent a defensive player is in terms of stopping ball carriers as an individual player.

- **Assisted tackles:** This is when a player is credited for helping another teammate or teammates successfully bring down the opposing ball carrier. In this case, both players involved are credited with a tackle. An assisted tackle can be awarded to more than one player; however, this is generally quite rare.

- **Tackles for loss:** These tackles are incredibly important and are achieved when a player tackles an opposing ball carrier behind the line of scrimmage; essentially, when this happens, the opposing team will lose yardage. For instance, if a team loses three yards due to a tackle for loss, they would then need to gain additional yardage to make up for it before their downs expire. Therefore, if it was their first down, they would now need to achieve a total of thirteen yards within the three remaining downs. Tackles for loss can be awarded as either a solo or an assisted tackle.

- **Sacks:** Sacks are the cream of the crop of tackles in football. A sack is when a player tackles the quarterback behind the line of scrimmage before they can make their pass or hand the ball off for a run play. Sacks are the most valuable tackles in football, as they generally result in the opposing team losing the most yards in a single play. If a sack is a result of an assisted tackle, then each player will be awarded half a sack on their stat sheet).

Tackling Form

Tackling is an art form and is not something players can just recklessly execute. To tackle well, a player needs to have excellent tackling form. Not only will great form lead to match-winning tackles, but they will also limit the risk of injury. (It also helps a player to have long arms, but it's not necessarily required for someone to be good at tackling.) Great tackling form for a football player includes:

- Ensure that their feet are shoulder-width apart and maintain a low center of gravity as they approach the ball carrier for a tackle.
- For an effective tackle, players need to resist the urge to drop their heads and instead keep their heads up and their eyes focused on their opponent's waist; this area is known as the "strike zone." When players tackle the midsection of an opposing player, it will minimize head contact and limit the risk of injury and the risk of being given a penalty by the referee.
- They need to keep their backs straight and avoid arching or bending them, as this could lead to an injury.
- A football player should wrap both their arms around the opposing player, preferably around their legs or waist, as this will ensure a secure hold and prevent the ball carrier from breaking free. This is essential for maintaining great tackling form.

- Players should pull their targets sharply toward them while lifting them slightly at the same time.
- Lastly, players need to explode through their hips and drive with their legs to generate power and momentum for a sublime tackle.

Tackling Angles

Angle tackling is key in football and is an extremely useful skill for a football player to have in their arsenal. Angle tackling is all about closing the gap between the defender and the ball carrier while still keeping control of their tackle. Think of it this way: When a defender intersects the path of a ball carrier, it gives their team the upper hand, as it will either push the opposing player toward the sideline or right in the path of pursuing defensive teammates.

An angle tackle is similar to a frontal tackle; the only major difference is that the defender will be approaching the ball carrier from the side to make a tackle. While it sounds pretty simple, in practice, there's a whole process defending players need to follow to get this skill right. To start with, players need to stay close to the ground when making an angle tackle and wrap the ball carrier with their helmet across the ball carrier's chest. Next on the checklist is to ensure that the defensive player keeps in front of the opposing player to avoid any nasty neck or head injuries. The aim here is for a defensive player to wrap their arms around their opponent's waist.

Once they've got their opponent wrapped up in their clutches, it's all about leverage. Defenders will need to lift the ball carrier as much as they can and chop at their feet. Once they feel in control, it's time to finish them off by bringing them down, whether it's to take them to the ground or move them out of bounds. It's an extremely useful tackle that's all about good technique and smart defensive instincts.

Tackling Strategies for Different Situations

Tackling takes all shapes and sizes during a game and often requires a defender to adapt to a game situation. Here are the three most common tackling strategies defenders need to employ during game time.

Open-Field Tackling

Open-field tackling is often considered one of the hardest skills to master as a defender, as this tackling scenario comes into play when the ball carrier has tons of open space and has room to maneuver, thus making it far easier for them to evade tacklers. However, defenders can still stop ball carriers with acres of open space by making use of proper pursuit angles and clever footwork to close down the distance between themselves and the ball carrier to make a controlled tackle in that open space.

If a defender gets their angles wrong, it can be a serious blunder, as it can often lead to missed tackles or the ball carrier breaking away for a big gain of yardage. The trick here is for defenders to stay disciplined and wait for the perfect moment to strike, like a lion hunting a zebra. Players need to remain patient, avoid rushing into plays, and resist being easily juked or deceived by the ball carrier's slick moves. It's a real test of agility, speed, and observational decision-making, requiring defenders to stay focused and anticipate the ball carrier's next move.

Gang Tackling

Gang tackling is when the defensive team coordinates their counter by utilizing multiple defenders simultaneously to put an end to the ball carrier's pursuit downfield.

Gang tackling relies on great communication and even better coordination. Each defender must stick to their assigned tackling lane and prevent the ball carrier from finding a gap or escaping the tackle. Making sure that their wrapping-up technique is executed to perfection is crucial, as it will ensure that the ball carrier is brought down even if the defender is faced with resilience from the offensive player. Great gang tackling is a sign of a well-oiled defense that works exceptionally well as a unit.

Goal-Line and Short-Yardage Situations

When a defender is faced with a goal-line and short-yardage tackling situation, they are required to stop the ball carrier from crossing the goal line or gaining the necessary yardage for a first down. In these situations, defenders need to be extra disciplined and focused. Any lapse in concentration could result in the opposing team scoring or making the necessary yardage from their first down, which can cause a lot of trouble for the defending team.

Defenders need to prioritize filling any gaps in the defense and maintaining gap integrity to limit the ball carrier from finding open space to exploit. A defender's tackling technique needs to be even more on point in these situations, as they need to ensure they wrap up the ball carrier securely to prevent any points being scored or yardage being made after contact. For goal-line and short-yardage situations, defenders will use the "Root Hog" technique; essentially, this means they will position their shoulder pads lower than those of the offensive linemen. This prevents the opposing offense from gaining control by denying them the chance to get underneath the defender. Maintaining a lower pad level grants the defense greater leverage and power necessary to disrupt offensive plays.

BLOCKING FUNDAMENTALS

Like tackling, blocking is another fundamental skill players must have in their repertoire. Remember the expression explained above, "we've got to cover our blocking and tackling"? Blocking is when a player physically obstructs an opposing player with their body to create space for their teammates, protect the ball carrier and passer from oncoming opposing defenders, and open running lanes for offensive running plays for their team.

Blocking Stance

Blocking is especially crucial for successful line play, and a player's stance will make a world of difference between a good block and a phenomenal one. Their stance affects everything, from the first step they take right up until they make that initial contact with a defender. A perfected stance will make a football player a force to be reckoned with on the field. Additionally, it will ensure they maintain their balance, gain leverage over their opponents, and confidently prepare them to engage physically with opposing players.

On the contrary, a poor stance can leave a player at a massive disadvantage. Offensive linemen generally assume a three-point stance, which means they have one hand on the ground and the other hand resting on their thigh or knee. This allows explosive power and swift movements as soon as they leave the line of scrimmage.

Maintaining a solid blocking stance requires attention and focus over a player's entire body. They need to be mindful of how they position their feet, right up to their head and upper body. A solid blocking stance includes

Feet

Players must ensure their feet are shoulder-width apart and distribute their weight evenly to enhance their balance. Next, they need to make sure they stand on the balls of their feet and that they are firmly rooted in the ground. Furthermore, they must resist the urge to lean forward or backward, as doing so could expose vulnerabilities that defenders could use against them, and this can put a player in an unfavorable starting position once the play has started.

Base

Football players must align their shoulders and knees while they stay square to the line of scrimmage. Furthermore, they stagger their feet from toe to instep and ensure their right foot is facing forward on the right and their left foot is facing forward on the left. When getting ready to block, players won't tilt or twist at all! If they do, savvy defenders could use this fault against them, especially for pulling linemen. This is because defenders could shoot the gap in the opposite direction a player is twisting and disrupt the play.

Hands and Elbows

Football players will keep their thumbs up and elbows in, and this simple form is crucial for a successful blocking stance! This will help maximize their striking power, as positioning their hands and thumbs upwards allows their elbows to naturally flow upwards, giving them extra power for their block.

Another trick players use is keeping their elbows tight against their bodies.

Head and Upper Body

Players must always keep their eyes on the prize and their heads back. A good stance requires players to never lead with their heads when they block, as this can cause a nasty injury. When preparing for a block, players pull their shoulders back and make sure they open up their chests for greater leverage.

Step and Strike

The action is about to begin! Players will take a six-inch step toward their opponent with their first step and cock their hand back as if they were a gunslinger while at the same time keeping their thumbs up and elbows in for their initial strike. Next, they will take another six-inch step toward the opponent for a venomous strike. They will unleash their gunslinging arms and strike the opponent around the chest area. Lastly, they'll keep their hips lower than their opponents to maintain leverage during the strike.

Finishing the Block

Now it's time for the grand finale. Players will drive their feet right up until they hear the refs whistle after making contact with their opponent. During the block, players will drive their opponents away from the ball and the heart of the play. Furthermore, they will not hesitate to ground their opponents for a successful finish.

Footwork

Having killer footwork is a must in football but even more so for the big men up front on the offensive line. These guys need to be nimble on their feet like a cat, using quick, short steps to maintain balance and keep up with the fast-moving defenders on the opposing team. They must stay square to the line of scrimmage and mirror the opposing defenders' every move.

Through footwork mastery, linemen can control the game and influence the direction in which the defenders move, thus opening up running lanes for the ball carrier and giving the quarterback time and options to make that epic play. Let me tell y'all that when those linemen's footwork is on point, they're like a brick wall out there, making it almost impossible for defenders to get through.

The trick is to stay light on your feet and react in the blink of an eye to whatever the defense throws at you. Fancy footwork isn't about showboating—it's the backbone of a solid offensive and sets the stage for match-winning plays!

Hand Placement

Hand placement during a block can make all the difference in gaining an advantage over a defender. Linemen typically target what is known as the "strike zone," which is the area between the defender's chest and shoulders, to maximize both control and power. They will position their hands inside the defender's shoulder pads to manipulate the defender's movements and redirect them away from the quarterback and ball carrier.

They do this by positioning their thumbs near the area where the shoulder pads are tied together, then using their remaining four fingers around the side to reach into the crevice near their opponent's armpit. Once they've got a good grip, they can use the defender's shoulder pads as a steering wheel, and bam! The defender will be theirs to manipulate and control.

CATCHING AND BALL HANDLING

Catching and ball handling are two of the most fundamental rules in football, and they do get the crowd buzzing when a beautiful catch is made. These skills are especially paramount for offensive players such as receivers, tight ends, and running backs. Simply put, catching is about snagging the football and keeping possession after the ball has been thrown by the quarterback, whether it's simply making an epic catch or running downfield for a touchdown once the catch has been made.

Catching and ball handling are what separate good players from game-winning players. Top-notch offensive players make sure their ball handling and catching skills are on the money to make serious yardage and score points for their team.

The Basics of Ball Handling

You may think catching sounds simple, but catching a football thrown at lightning speed with defenders out for blood and putting pressure on you in every direction is no easy feat. It takes a lot of focus, hard work, and, most importantly, good form to make a game-winning catch; hell, even a catch without such high stakes can be difficult.

Hand and Body Positioning

So, here's the thing: no two passes in football are the same, and despite what people may say, no pass in the NFL is a walk in the park either. One pass may come straight at you, another pass may go off to the side, and let's not even get into those crazy yet oh-so-satisfying Hail Marys that come out of nowhere (for the newbies – a Hail Mary is a very long pass, usually thrown as a last-ditch effort to score a touchdown). But no matter the pass or the situation, there are some techniques all players can follow to make catching just that little bit easier. These techniques include:

- **Body positioning:** First off, players square their shoulders and position themselves so that they are facing the quarterback; however, that isn't always possible, but it makes a big difference. Besides facing the quarterback, they will also need to focus on the ball's trajectory and align their bodies so that they position themselves directly within the ball's flight path. Body positioning is crucial for a receiver to increase their chances of catching passes from their quarterback.

- **Hand positioning:** A player will position their hands based on how and where the ball is being thrown. If it's a high pass, then they'll extend their arms and form a diamond shape using their index fingers and thumb. This is a common technique receivers typically use. Additionally, receivers will often position their hands slightly in front of their bodies with their fingers spread and their palms facing toward the incoming ball, as this will help cushion the catch. For low passes, a player's hand positioning is a little different. A receiver will cup their hands in front of them by putting their pinky fingers together to catch tricky low passes.

- **Tucking the ball:** Once a player has received and controlled the football after a completed pass, they will need to protect it from those blood-thirsty defenders. Once the catch is made, the receiver will use their hand, forearm, and elbow to press the ball firmly against their body and tuck it in nice and tight. Additionally, they will keep the football relatively high and close to their body so they can protect the football as they run to the end zone to score a game-winning touchdown.

Route Running and Stems

Running is somewhat like an art form in football, and route running is the backbone of any great play. Route running demands precise movements and strategic patterns from offensive football players to outwit opposing defenses and create opportunities for receptions. (Pay attention Taylor Swift fans

– exceptional route running is what makes Travis Kelce a superstar).

It is up to the receivers to master an assortment of running techniques, such as cuts, breaks, and releases, to establish passing windows for the quarterback and to leave defenders utterly confuzzled. A central focus of route running is route stems. Route stems are used to dictate how a receiver will initiate their running route off the line of scrimmage and are pivotal for clever plays.

Route stems come in various forms, from straight runs that will maintain a vertical threat to defenses to curved approaches that bring forth an air of unpredictability. Receivers may adjust their stems by altering the speed and depth of their runs to deceive defenders while also setting up opponents for subsequent route breaks.

Route stems are one of the most strategic tools in a football team's arsenal and allow receivers to completely manipulate defenders and gain valuable leverage before they have even made their intended route cut.

Ultimately, the success of route running relies on the receiver's skill to maintain balance, execute killer footwork, and masterful running techniques throughout the stem. In doing so, they can ensure they can execute precise breaks and remain in control of their route. Route stems and route running are crucial for receivers as they aim to create separation and capitalize on scoring opportunities for their team's passing game.

Ball Security Techniques

Now that a player has the football in their hands, there is only one thing on their minds, and that's to score a touchdown, baby! However, to pull that off, they need to have expert ball security. Ball security is exactly what it sounds like: securing the ball from the opposition and making sure it doesn't exchange hands. Whether the ball is being carried by a running back or a receiver, knowing how to hold and run with the football will make the difference between keeping possession and turning it over.

For starters, the minute a player gets ahold of the ball, they need to keep that sucker real close! The ball becomes their most prized possession. They need to tuck it snugly, right under their ribs. Additionally, a player can also press it tight against their chest, but more importantly, they need to hold it tight as their life depends on it. Ball security requires a player to hold the ball high, not by their waists; holding it high acts as a great defense against defenders with sticky fingers who want to strip the football away from the ball carrier.

In addition to carrying the ball tight and high, players need to ensure that they also :

- Grip the front tip of the football with their fingers or palms and make sure it is securely covered.
  Depending on a player's build, the way they choose to grip the ball may differ.
- Press the outside panel of the football against their forearm and position the fingers of their ball-carrying hand towards their body.
- To position the ball securely on the inside panel, players press it against their ribs, holding it slightly

forward on their abdomen. They keep their elbows close to their body and conceal the back side of the football to prevent opposing players from punching it out.

- Lastly, they place the hand that isn't carrying the football on top of the ball, as this will add a fourth point of contact for that extra bit of safety insurance.

Keep in mind that sometimes players need to switch things up and use both hands when carrying the football. For instance, when a player is driving into a crowd of defenders, they will need to hold the football close to their body and keep their arms wrapped around it. In other instances, a player may need to switch hands on the fly, and when they do, they need to make sure that they do it away from the defense. Essentially, when that ball is in their possession, they have to make sure it stays in their possession no matter the cost.

We've covered the skills a player needs, but football is a team sport, so it is imperative that we explore the different team units and positions that make up a football team's roster.

CHAPTER 4

Team Units and Positions

In football, there are loads of positions—24, to be exact! At any given time, there will be 22 players on the field, with each team either fielding eleven of their offensive players or defensive players, depending on whether a team is playing offensively or defensively based on the game situation. An NFL team will have approximately 50 players in a squad.

TEAM COMPOSITION: OFFENSE, DEFENSE, AND SPECIAL TEAMS

In football, teams are divided into specific units. As mentioned in Chapter 2, teams will have offensive and defensive units, but that's not all; they will also have a special unit.

The diagrams below include a basic visual representation of where the different positions "line up" on the football field. Different plays, which can be thought of as strategies or plans of action, can have slightly different formations for the players. For example, you might see two tight ends and only one running back for certain offensive plays, but these pictures give you a general idea of who stands where on the field.

The line of scrimmage would be located directly between these two diagrams:

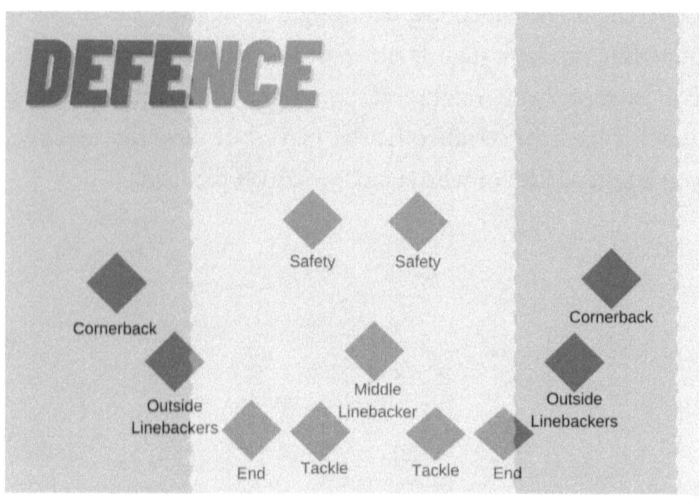

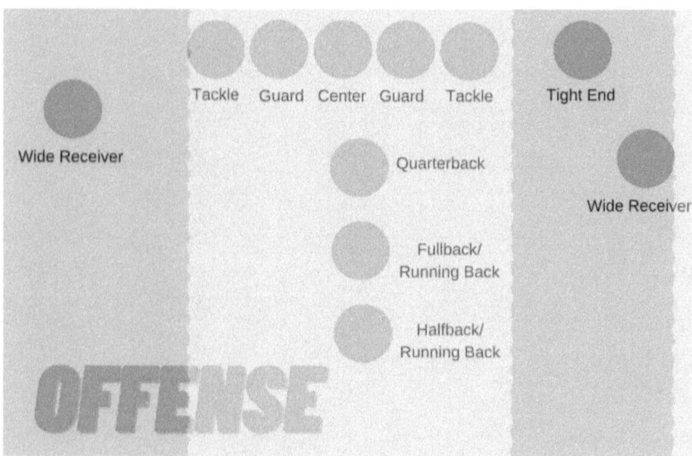

Offensive Unit

The offensive unit consists of 11 players, and within these 11 players, they are further divided into two main groups: linemen and everybody else. The offensive linemen are made up of six positions: left tackle, left guard, right guard, right tackle, and center. These guys are responsible for a crucial task, which is to protect the quarterback at all costs and create openings for the ball carrier by blocking opposing defenders. Ultimately, the linemen need to ensure a solid line of defense to make sure that their teammates can execute game-winning plays by making openings for them.

The remaining offense consists of six players in total. These include wide receivers, tight ends, the quarterback, and running backs. These guys make those magic plays and move the football downfield through running and passing plays to make valuable yardage. The backs and receivers need insane agility and lightning speed to evade opposing defenders to make yardage, score points, and be the primary cog in their team's offensive strategy.

Defensive Unit

As mentioned in Chapter 2, the job of the defensive unit is to put an end to the efforts of the opposing offense through tackling, interceptions, forcing fumbles, and any other means necessary. These guys will take to the field when the opposing team has possession of the football, and their primary objective is to stop the other team from scoring points and gaining yards.

The defensive unit consists of eleven players and is divided into three main categories of players:

- **The defensive line:** The defensive line consists of formidable athletes who are positioned at the line of scrimmage. The line of scrimmage can be understood as an imaginary line that stretches for the length of the field and is a line that cannot be crossed until the next play has started. The defensive line is responsible for putting pressure on the quarterback and nullifying running plays.
- **Linebackers:** They play behind or to the outside of the defensive line and excel at blitzing (disrupting passing plays by the offense), tackling, and overall pass defense.
- **Secondary:** This unit comprises safeties and cornerbacks, and acts as the last line of defense. They mainly focus on pass coverage; however, they also aid in tackling if the runners make it through the linebackers.

Special Unit

Finally, we have the special unit, also referred to as special teams. This distinct unit may not see as much action as the other two units, but trust me, they are just as important to put some invaluable points on the board. The special unit is responsible for handling kicking plays and is made up of positions such as the snapper, blockers, holder, placekicker, jammers, punters, punt protectors, punt returners, and gunners. Typically, these guys will be called onto the field whenever their side needs to kick at the goalposts or return the football to the opposing team. In most cases, when one special team takes to the field, the opposing special team will follow suit.

Many people downplay the importance of the special team, but if a team needs some clutch points, these are your guys. They are crucial in determining field position and scoring opportunities, especially when it comes to field goals and extra points. Each unit has a role to play, and when they work in tandem together, they become a force to be reckoned with!

ROLES AND RESPONSIBILITIES OF DIFFERENT POSITIONS

Unlike most team sports like soccer, basketball, hockey, or volleyball, where teams attack and defend simultaneously, football is unique as teams will never attack and defend at the same time. You'll never find both teams' offenses on the field at the same time, nor will you find both teams' defensive sides on the field at the same time.

Football teams alternate between offense and defense based on which team has possession of the football, and once the ball changes hands, teams will alternate units accordingly. Football's unique dynamic gameplay ensures constant strategic shifts and play styles depending on the game's situation, thus requiring teams to excel both offensively and defensively to win games.

Offensive Positions

In the offensive unit, there are eight different positions, each with its own set of roles and responsibilities they need to adhere to and execute. These positions include

Centers

The center makes up part of the offensive line, and although they may not get as much glory as a quarterback, their contribution to their team's offense cannot be understated. Each team has one center and it is their responsibility to pass the ball between his legs in a move known as a "snap." Snapping the ball between their legs is what starts a play in football. Typically, once these unsung heroes snap the ball back, they transition to blocking duties.

The center plays a crucial role when it comes to communication, and often, their decision-making in terms of defensive alignments and counterstrategies can either make or break a play. Their responsibilities include snapping the ball back to the quarterback at the beginning of the play, protecting the quarterback from oncoming defenders, communicating strategies, and playing with their fellow linemen. Ever heard stuff like hike 32, 18, hike? Well, that is when the quarterback is giving commands to the center regarding the play the team will make once the center snaps the ball. Some of the greatest

NFL centers in history include Jim Otto, Jim Langer, Dwight Stephenson, and Jason Kelce.

Tackle

Moving on to the big guys on the front line, we've got the tackles. There are two tackles in a football team: the left tackle and the right tackle. Their primary role is blocking, blocking, and even more blocking! These giant athletes line up next to the guards and are ready to give everything they have to shield the quarterback from danger and open up lanes for the running backs to exploit and make some serious yardage.

As the age-old question goes, does size matter? Well, as a tackle, it certainly does. The bigger, the better. In this case, tackles are some of the largest players on the football field, often weighing over 300 pounds and towering well over six feet tall. But let's not get it twisted. Being big is great and all, but it's not everything. These behemoths need to be quick on their feet, too, shifting their weight from side to side to shut down opposing defenders.

To reiterate, there are two tackles in an offensive unit; this includes the left tackle and the right tackle. The left tackle's job is to guard the quarterback's blindside, while the right tackle's job is to clear lanes and create space for killer passes and lightning-fast running plays. There have been countless talented tackles in the NFL, but names like Ron Mix, Lou Creekmur, Anthony Munoz, and Forrest Greg immediately come to mind.

Guards

Guards are similar to tackles; they are the beefy blockers that operate in the trenches and are positioned on either side of the center. They form part of the linemen, and each football team has two of them. Their main gig is keeping those pesky defenders at bay, making inroads for their teammates to run through, or creating openings for a precision pass to make great yardage or score big.

These guys are the muscle of the linemen and often tip the scale at over 250 pounds. While they may be big men, don't let their size fool you; they are super nimble, too. The two guards include the left guard and the right guard. The left guard is responsible for protecting the quarterback's blind side from any defender trying to gatecrash the party, similar to the left tackle, while the right guard is responsible for holding down the fort on the other side, creating running opportunities for their teammates by throwing blocks left, right, and center, and bulldozing through defensive players. Some of the greatest guards in NFL history include Larry Allen, Gene Upshaw, John Hannah, and Steve Hutchinson.

Tight End

Tight ends are those all-around maestros that are simply great at everything. In saying that, it is also one of the most difficult positions in football. They need to be great at blocking, running, and catching. These athletes have it all and possess a mix of brute strength, athleticism, and finesse. There is only one, or sometimes two tight end players in an offensive lineup and they bridge the gap between the offensive linemen and the wide receivers.

When it comes to running plays, these guys throw down in the trenches, laying sublime blocks and paving a route for their teammates to do their thang as they race downfield. But don't underestimate their catching skills. They're as lethal in the passing game, snagging short bursts of yardage and moving the chains in the offense as they are at blocking. These guys are the unsung heroes of the offense and many teams' secret weapon; they do the dirty work while still making big plays when it matters. Tight ends are exciting players to watch, but some of the most exciting tight ends include legends such as Rob Gronkowski, Travis Kelce, Tony Gonzalez, and Antonio Gates.

Running Backs

Running backs are some of the most exciting players to most fans, and for good reason. They are the powerhouses of the offense who thrive on their electric speed as they run downfield to create options for the quarterback and make some invaluable yardage for their team.

Whenever the game is on the line, it's the running back's time to shine! They are the masters of the ground game and use their lightning speed, overpowering strength, and cat-like agility to navigate the gaps in the defense.

Whether it be a pass play or a handoff from the quarterback, these athletes seem to always know how to make magic happen; they are like the engine that drives the offense forward, finding holes in the defense, breaking down tackles, and running downfield for that much-needed touchdown!

There are usually one or two running backs on the football field at a time, and they are divided into two different positions: fullbacks and halfbacks (also known as tailbacks). It is the fullback's job to use their muscle to clear a path for their speedier counterparts, while the halfbacks will make use of their agility to dance through the opposing defense to find open space and make big and important yardage for their team. Running backs always know how to get a crowd going, but players like Jim Brown, Walter Payton, Barry Sanders, Emmitt Smith, Adrian Peterson, and Jerome Bettis always seemed to bring their A-game!

Quarterback

The superstars of football and arguably the most important position on the team. They are the heartbeat of any offensive side; they are like the conductor of this orchestra we call football. Their job is to orchestrate the team's movement on the field and unleash a beautiful pass to make the yardage that wins games.

With every snap, the quarterback carries the weight of the strategic decisions of the play, such as whether they should launch a magical pass downfield or take matters into their own hands and scramble for yardage. The key to a quarterback's success is their keen eyes, which allow them to scan the entire field, analyze defensive formations, and spot open receivers even amidst the chaos of oncoming defenders gunning for them. A quarterback's ability to make quick and effective decisions can win or lose their team a game. These superstars dictate the flow of the offense and shape how every play will roll out.

If that wasn't enough, quarterbacks need to possess exceptional leadership skills as they hold so much responsibility on the field, and of course, they need to exhibit pinpoint accuracy with their passes. They rally the team during hairy moments and inspire greatness with every throw they make. They may be the superstars everyone is watching on the field, but it comes with a mountain of pressure. When quarterbacks come up in a discussion, I guarantee these four names come up every time: Joe Montana, Peyton Manning, Patrick Mahomes, and, of course, Tom Brady! (Side note for newbies: most football fans seem to either really love, or really hate Tom Brady. It probably depends mostly on whether or not he dashed their own team's hopes at a crucial moment in history...but regardless, his stats speak for themselves.)

Wide Receivers

The last warriors on a football team's offensive unit are none other than those exciting wide receivers. There are generally two wide receivers in an offensive lineup, and they are at the heart of the passing plays. It's up to them to snatch up those pinpoint aerial deliveries from the quarterback and make that final dash to the end zone once they've made the catch.

Their biggest assets are their lightning speed, superhuman agility, and towering frames. (If you're a soccer or rugby fan, they are the closest thing to a winger like Kylian Mbappe or Cheslin Kolbe, ready to burst into action along the sidelines.) However, none of those things matter if a receivers can't catch the ball.

This position demands precision and explosiveness as they navigate their way through the opposing defense and create passing opportunities for the quarterback. As they run down their chosen routes, their eyes are fixed on one thing, and that's the end zone as they wait for the perfect moment to make their move to put points on the board.

While running and catching are their main jobs, they sometimes need to act as blockers during running plays to shield their teammates from defensive players so the running backs can do their thang. Some of the best wide receivers to grace the game include Jerry Rice and Justin Jefferson (Griffiths, 2023b).

Defensive Positions

In the defensive unit, 11 players are divided into three subunits: the defensive line, linebackers, and the secondary unit. Each of these subunits has its own set of roles and responsibilities. These defensive positions consist of:

Defensive Ends

There are two defensive ends, and these guys are the guardians of any good defensive line. They are stationed at the outer edges of the defense and unleash utter chaos on the opposing offensive side. Their main role is to put a stop to running backs from gaining yards along the sidelines of the field. They are also responsible for achieving a satisfying sack on the quarterback.

They are true athletes who combine both brute strength and electrifying speed. They truly are a force of nature on the field, as they disrupt offensive plays and inflict tackles that truly leave their mark on the opposing team. It is their agility that allows them to swiftly navigate through the offensive line, while their brute strength helps them bring down even the most resilient ball carriers. When talking about iconic defensive ends, Jared Allen and Reggie White will always come up.

Defensive Tackles

There are two defensive tackles in a defensive lineup. They are stationed at the heart of the defensive line. They don't have it easy and are constantly facing a barrage of pressure from the opposing offensive linemen, who are doing everything they can to put an end to the defensive tackles' efforts.

It is their unwavering tenacity and raw power that truly set them apart. It is their job to fend off the double-team blocks from opposing offenses as they tirelessly pursue the opposing team's ball carrier. Defensive tackles disrupt opposing running plays that come up through the middle with their superhuman power and relentless strength of will. Their secret weapon is their ability to penetrate the line of scrimmage and put as much pressure as humanly possible on the quarterback. Legendary defensive ends include big-name superstars such as Warren Sapp and Alan Page.

Nose Tackle

The last position in the defensive line unit is the nose tackle. Nose tackles serve as the linchpin of a defensive unit and are stationed right in the epicenter of the defensive line. There is only one nose tackle in a defensive lineup, and they are typically deployed in the heart of a 3–4 defensive alignment. However, the offensive team doesn't make it easy for these unsung defensive heroes, as nose tackles often face a relentless onslaught from opposing offensive linemen seeking to disrupt their presence.

This position is best known for players with a crazy amount of resolve and unyielding toughness, as they are required to endure a barrage of mega hits coming from every direction, epitomizing the grit and determination required to excel in this position.

Their main objective is to act as the anchor for the defensive unit in the front line, putting an end to running plays coming up the middle and placing immense pressure on the quarterback. Being on the frontline of defense, they play a key role in dictating the pace of the game and have the opportunity to shift momentum in favor of their team. Some of the greatest nose tackles in NFL history include Fred Smerlas, Ted Washington, Jim Burt, and Dontari Poe.

Linebackers (Outside and Inside, or Middle Linebackers)

Linebackers form the defensive unit and are positioned just behind the defensive line. These guys are the frontline defenders, and their job is to block and tackle those speedy running backs, in addition to penetrating the offensive line. Linebackers are super agile, incredibly powerful, and extremely fast to boot. These qualities are essential when engaging in the heat of play against the opposing offense. Generally, there will be three or four linebackers on the field at once. Among the linebackers, a team will field inside or middle linebackers and outside linebackers.

The middle linebackers assume the leadership role in this defensive unit, as they will orchestrate defensive strategies and play-calling, showcasing their tactical prowess and experience. Generally, the standard is to deploy a three-linebacker formation with two outside linebackers and one inside or middle linebacker; however, this sometimes differs based on a team's strategy.

The job of an outside linebacker includes penetrating the offensive line, placing pressure on the quarterback, and, if possible, pulling off a sack. These defensive players excel at containing runs along the sidelines, which in turn will force the running backs to try their luck through the central defense. Outside linebackers are generally taller and leaner in physique; this build is ideal for disrupting passes as well as pursuing and tackling quarterbacks with quick feet.

As for the inside or middle linebackers, they are stationed centrally; they are responsible for mitigating offensive runs that come through the middle and helping defend against passes. While they may not be as tall as outside linemen, they are usually bulkier than them, which helps facilitate impactful tackles on fast-moving running backs. Football fans have been treated to loads of talented linemen, names that come to mind for outside linebackers include Jack Ham, Bobby Bell, and Derrick Thomas, but if we are talking about middle linemen, then legends like Ray Nitschke, Luke Kuechly, and Dick Butkus were up there with the very best.

Safeties and Cornerbacks

The last unit of the defensive lineup is the defensive back, also known as the "safety." This unit consists of cornerbacks and safeties.

Cornerbacks typically go head-to-head with the opposing wide receivers, and it is their job to stop any pass receptions by tightly guarding them. Their other responsibilities include tackling running backs and provoking turnovers through powerful tackles and sly interceptions. Some of the best cornerbacks of all time include Deion Sanders, Ronnie Lott, Dick "Night Train" Lane, Darrell Green, Rod Woodson, and Mel Blount.

The second position that makes up the defensive back is the safety. There are two safety positions: the free safety and the strong safety, and they act as the ultimate defensive bulwark. These guys are positioned closest to their team's end zone, making them the last line of defense. Effective communication and swift reactions are extremely desirable traits for a safety.

Strong safeties align themselves on the field's "strong side," opposite the tight end. They are known for their robustness, and they challenge charging running backs head-on with unbreakable resolve. They often rely on their strength and size to put a stop to the opposition's advances. Strong safeties such as John Lynch, Dennis Smith, Ken Houston, and Troy Polamalu were legendary.

As for the free safeties, they are positioned on the "weak side," which is the side of the field without a tight end. They are generally faster and lighter than strong safeties; therefore, their focus lies more on disrupting their opponent's passing game. They are the last line of defense, so interceptions, disrupting the flow of the opposing passing game, and reading the quarterback's intent are key responsibilities of theirs. Some of the best to grace the NFL include Paul Krause, Ed Reed, and Yale Lary.

Defensive Coverage

In football, defensive coverage is an important strategic aspect of the defense, and teams employ a variety of coverage schemes to defend against passing plays. These include:

- **Man coverage:** In this defensive strategy, defenders are required to cover specific offensive players, generally with man-to-man guarding. To pull this off, each defender essentially shadows an appointed receiver to deny them space and disrupt any pass attempts.
- **Zone coverage:** For this coverage scheme, rather than being assigned players to guard, defensive players will be assigned zones on the field to cover. Covering areas rather than plays allows them to react to passes and provide support to fellow defensive teammates if needed.
- **Zone match coverage:** Here, defenders will combine elements from both man and zone coverage. Defenders will initially cover an appointed zone; however, they will transition to man-to-man

coverage if a receiver enters their zone. This ensures tighter coverage.

- **Man match coverage:** This is another hybrid coverage scheme, a defender will be assigned a specific offensive player to cover. However, they will be given the flexibility to adjust the receiver's movements. If their assigned defender drifts into another defender's zone, they may pick another player to cover. Man-match coverage blends man-to-man and zone coverage principles dynamically.

Special Team Positions

As I said earlier, the special team may not get all the glory, but that does not make them any less important. These guys have won loads of matches for their teams through field goals and extra points that have made all the difference. The special team is made up of nine positions, which include:

The Kicker

The kicker can easily be your potential match-winner and is the hero of the special team. He is tasked with the important task of splitting the uprights for field goals and adding the crucial extra point after a touchdown. These guys are also responsible for the kickoff. Some of the best kickers in NFL history include Justin Tucker, Morten Anderson, and Lou Graza.

Return Specialist

These guys are the dynamo of the special teams; they are skilled at snatching kickoffs and punts as well as blazing downfield, sprinting their butts off toward the end zone, and evading tackles with every step they take.

Kick Returner

The kick returner is like a flash of lightning on kickoffs, ready to grab the ball and electrify the crowd with a swift sprint toward the end zone, leaving defenders scrambling in their wake.

Punt Returner

These guys are the masters of finesse and are responsible for fielding punts as well as deciding if they should make a daring return or signal a fair catch, and of course, this is all being done while opposing defenders are rushing at them.

Punter

The punter is the strategic mastermind of the special team, they are called to the field to give a booming punt downfield when their team's offense has stalled. They need to punt with both power and precision to ensure the ball lands deep in the opposition's territory.

Long Snapper

These guys work in tandem with the punter; it is their job to deliver a snap with pinpoint precision to the punter to ensure every punt goes off smoothly.

Holder

The holder works with the kicker; they need to have steady hands as that's what will set the stage for an awesome kick from the kicker. The holder secures the ball and holds it in the perfect position for a successful field goal or extra point.

Gunner

These are the speedsters of the special team. Their job is to run downfield as fast as humanly possible to place pressure on the opposing returner/punter and disrupt their rhythm to prevent any hope of a big play.

Personal Protector (AKA the Upback)

Their job is simple: to protect the punter. They need to be ready to shield against any onrushing defenders and occasionally spring a surprise play when least expected.

POSITIONAL UNIFORM NUMBERS

A player's number is more than a number—it is tied to their position. In the NFL, certain numbers indicate certain positions, as this helps the referee determine who is and who isn't allowed to catch the ball. The following numbers are worn by specific positions:

- 0 to 19 are worn by quarterbacks
- 0 to 49 and 90 to 99 are worn by punters and kickers
- 0 to 49 are reserved for defensive backs
- 0 to 49 and 80 to 89 are reserved for running backs
- 0 to 49 and 80 to 89 are worn by tight ends
- 0 to 49 and 80 to 89 are reserved for offensive lineman
- 0 to 59 and 90 to 99 are worn by linebackers
- 50 to 79 are reserved for offensive lineman
- 50 to 79 and 90 to 99 are worn by defensive linemen

These jersey numbers are the official position numbers as of the 2023 NFL season and the seasons that follow.

So, there we have it. A football team is made up of an offensive unit, a defensive unit, and a special team, with each unit consisting of various positions. Next up, we will tackle the rules of the game.

CHAPTER 5

The Rules of Football

Between 1974 and 2011, the NFL made changes to the kickoff line three times. Each change was in response to particular circumstances and trends of the era in which it was made. In 1974, the kickoff line was moved from the 40-yard line to the 35-yard line as the NFL wanted to increase the number of exciting returns; this immediately boosted return rates from 75% to 92%. Then, in 1994, the NFL shifted the kickoff line even closer from the 35-yard line to the 30-yard line; this increased return rates from 68% to 88% from the previous season. Finally, in 2011, the NFL moved the kickoff line back to the 35-yard line to reduce running starts as concussions and injuries were becoming more common in the NFL. This new change saw a 40% drop in concussions as well as an approximate decrease in return rates of 50% (Holder, 2023).

PENALTIES AND INFRACTIONS

Alright team, we covered all the primary objectives of the game in Chapter 2. However, what about the nitty-gritty stuff like penalties and infringements? Knowing the basics of the game is one thing, but knowing important rules, like when a team is penalized or when a player is blown for infringements, are important aspects of football we need to consider.

In football, a penalty can cause a real roadblock on a team's path to victory. A penalty is when a team violates certain rules. When this happens, the ref will blow their whistle and call a foul, and a penalty will be given. Penalties can seriously damage a team in a variety of ways, such as loss of yardage from 5 to 15 yards, loss of a down, automatic first downs, and, in extreme cases, even player ejections.

For instance, if a team gets a 10-yard penalty on first and ten, it will now be first and twenty. Mistakes happen, but too many mistakes will catch up to a team, and generally, the team that makes the fewest mistakes and racks up the fewest penalties often wins. Referees will signal a penalty by either hoisting up a yellow flag or using hand gestures to signal a penalty. Here are common penalties and infringements commonly found in a football game:

- **Blocking below the waist:** This is when a player executes a block on another player below their waistline, as this can cause significant injuries, particularly to a player's knees. This will typically result in a loss of 10 yards. This penalty is intended to ensure player safety and maintain the integrity of football.

- **Block from behind:** Another blocking foul is when a block is made from behind a player's back, as it runs the risk of serious injury and provides an unfair advantage to the blocking team. Generally, this will result in around a 10-yard penalty, which can seriously impact a favorable field position and impact the momentum of a game. All blocks in football need to be made from the front.

- **Chop block:** A chop block is when one player blocks high while another player blocks low simultaneously. A chop block will cause an opposing player to lose balance and can lead to serious injuries. Therefore, a chop block penalty often results in a team losing around 15 yards due to its vicious and dangerous nature.

- **Clipping:** This is one of the most serious fouls in football and is when a player blocks a player below the waist and from behind, which runs the risk of causing serious injuries, especially to a player's knees. NFL officials strictly enforce a 15-yard penalty for this infringement due to its severity and the risk it poses. In doing so, officials ensure player safety and maintain fair competition.

- **Delay of game:** This is when the center fails to snap the ball back before the play clock runs out. It is enforced as it disrupts the flow of the game and can hinder a team's momentum. While not as serious as the other fouls, it still results in a loss of five yards, which negatively impacts field position and could potentially influence the game's final result.

- **Holding:** This is when a player grabs another player's jersey or equipment (such as the helmet) to stop a player in their tracks. This common foul hinders fair competition and results in many penalties where the offender's team will lose 10 yards. If it is the defensive team that is called for holding, the offensive team will gain 5 yards and be awarded an automatic first down.

- **Pass interference:** This is a defensive foul when a defender restricts a receiver from catching the football by making contact with the player before the ball arrives. It is a crucial penalty that referees need to strictly enforce, as it can seriously influence the outcome of a passing play. Based on the severity of the pass interference, the ref will make a judgment call about whether to award the offensive team 10 yards or to let the offensive team start their first down at the spot where the interference took place, which can lead to a serious gain in yardage for the offensive team.

- **Roughing the passer/kicker:** This is one of the most critical penalties for referees to call due to the potential impact on the game and the safety of players. This foul is called when a defensive player makes unnecessary and malicious contact with a quarterback, punter, or kicker after the ball has already been launched or kicked. This is a serious violation and will result in a 15-yard gain penalty for the offense, and in severe cases, the defensive player may be ejected from the game.

- **Unsportsmanlike conduct:** Football may be played by big-buff guys, but that does not mean they are brutes; there is etiquette and sportsmanship that need to be adhered to on the football field. These fouls are called for any actions that violate the spirit of fair play and sportsmanship. In rare cases, if constant unsportsmanlike conduct persists from a singular player, they may be ejected from the game. Also, roughhousing with the officials is strictly out of the question. These fouls will result in an approximate loss of 15 yards. This may seem harsh, but it is what upholds sportsmanship and integrity in football. After all, millions of kids watch every game and view these football players as role models.

- **Encroachment:** This penalty is when a defensive player gets a little too excited and crosses the line of scrimmage before the center snaps the football; therefore, the offense starts with a disadvantage. Typically, this will result in the offensive team gaining an additional five yards.

- **False start:** In contrast, a false start is when offensive players jump the gun and move prematurely before the center snaps the ball. In this instance, the offense will lose five yards, putting their team in an unfavorable field position.

- **Offside:** The ref will blow for offside if any part of a player's body (offensive or defensive player) moves beyond the line of scrimmage before the football is snapped. This typically results in the offending team either losing five yards (if an offensive player was offside) or gaining five yards (if a defensive player was offside).

- **Personal foul:** A personal foul is when a player commits a severe infraction of the rules that endangers another player's safety. The offender's team will either lose or gain 15 yards, depending on whether it was an offensive or defensive personal foul.

I'm sure you've all noticed a trend here: If an offensive player commits a foul, their team will lose yards; if a defensive player is blown for a foul, then the offensive team will gain yards. Additionally, unlike in basketball or other team sports, penalties do not accumulate for individual players. In football, every foul called is imposed on the entire team, so players need to keep their discipline on point for the sake of their team.

UNDERSTANDING RULE ENFORCEMENT

The NFL doesn't just change rules willy-nilly, nope. The NFL's rule-making process undergoes a collaborative and thorough effort to improve the game for players, fans, and the sport itself. Football rules can only be altered by The Competition Committee, which is made up of representatives from across the league. It is their job to meticulously review various aspects of the sport every season by going over factors such as playing rules and player safety measures. Additionally, they also consider the input from franchises, football experts, league committees, players, the NFL Players Association, and various other opinions. They gather the queries from all these sources through surveys and in-depth discussions.

Once The Competition Committee has compiled all the relevant findings based on the previous season, they will then present their findings to the team owners at an annual meeting with all relevant football bodies present. They will discuss proposed rule changes and put the decision to a vote; however, for these new rules to be enforced, the proposed rule change will need to receive the support of at least 75% of the owners to take action. This annual process is in place to ensure that the NFL remains both responsive and dynamic to the ever-evolving needs of football while still maintaining the sport's core values of fairness, competitiveness, and player safety (NFL Football Operations, 2023)

THE BEST RULE CHANGES IN NFL HISTORY

The rules of football are constantly being tweaked, and for the most part, it has made the sport better and better with every change. The Competition Committee has done an excellent job over the years in maintaining football's integrity, adapting to the evolving trends of the era, and maintaining football's golden values of entertainment, fair play, competitiveness, and player safety. Over the countless changes the NFL has undergone over its illustrious history, these five rule changes were the best modifications to the sport in NFL history.

The Legalization of the Forward Pass

It wasn't until 1906 that the forward pass was legalized in football, and this drastic rule change would forever revolutionize football. Imagine football without forward passes; there would be no Tom Brady, Peyton Manning, Patrick Mahomes, or Joe Montana to light up a stadium with pinpoint passes and game-changing plays!

As mentioned in Chapter One, football was predominantly a ground-based game where passing was almost nonexistent; however, after 1906, all that changed, and the forward pass became a destructive weapon in a football team's offensive arsenal, opening a world of possibilities for offensive innovation and killer plays. Once the forward pass was legalized in football, quarterbacks quickly emerged as the stars of the show and one of, if not the, most important players on the field. The forward pass revolutionized aerial combat in football, igniting the excitement of fans with deep throws and precision passes from legendary quarterbacks.

The Point Increase for Touchdowns and the Point Decrease for Field Goals

Even earlier than the legalization of the forward pass was another revolutionary rule change. Between 1898 and 1912, the value of a touchdown increased from four to six points, while field goals decreased in value from five to three points between the years 1904 and 1909.

These point changes drastically altered the scoring dynamic of football. This rule change made teams strive to score more and more touchdowns rather than settle for field goals. This change in approach meant that teams would execute more aggressive offensive strategies and place higher priorities on their playmakers, who could cut through defenses and find the end zone with consistency.

The Five-Yard Contact Rule for Defenders

Fast forward several decades to 1978, and football introduced another monumental change known as the five-yard contact rule for defenders. This rule change was a game-changing moment for the passing game. The five-yard contact rule for defenders limited a defender's ability to cut off and impede receivers beyond the line of scrimmage. This change was enforced as the NFL wanted to improve the freedom of offensive lines and promote aerial plays to excite the crowd. This new rule changed everything and was the catalyst for high-octane passing offenses that prided themselves on explosive passing plays and dynamic receiver routes.

Instant Replays

In 1999, yet another revolutionary rule would be enforced, and this was the moment when technology and football intertwined. The instant replay was a significant step forward for officials to make accurate and fair calls. Instant replays provided NFL officials with an opportunity to review critical plays and reevaluate the calls they made to ensure they were correct. While instant replays have faced some challenges and controversies, overall, it was a monumental change that led to increased confidence in the integrity of the sport, and its impact on enhancing officiating standards can't be disputed.

Unlimited Substitutions

Lastly, we have unlimited substitutions, which was a new rule enforced in 1950 and would forever revolutionize the way football teams prioritized specialization and depth in their rosters. This change meant teams were no longer constrained to a set number of substitutions; thus, coaches were gifted with the flexibility to deploy specialized players and team units that were perfectly suited for specific game situations. Not only did this rule enhance player safety, as it gave players a chance to rest, but it also ushered in a new wave of strategic innovation and creative team management that the sport had never seen before.

While there have been many rule changes over the years, these five alterations shaped football into the sport we know and love today!

UNDERSTANDING THE NFL OFFICIALS

We've spoken a lot about the players, how they operate on the field, and their roles and responsibilities, but what about the officials who keep the game flowing and ensure a fair and competitive competition? Rules are there for a reason: to keep players safe and to keep the game interesting, and the ones who are making sure that happens are the seven officials on the field. In every game, seven NFL officials keep the game in check. These officials include the following:

Referee

The referee is the head honcho of the seven officials; you can find him positioned behind the offensive team. Furthermore, the ref will be wearing a white hat while all other officials wear a black hat.

Responsibilities

- counts the number of offensive players to ensure the correct amount is on the field
- observes the quarterback closely during passing plays
- during running plays, he monitors the running backs

- during a kicking play, he watches the kicker and the holder
- blows for penalties
- makes announcements for penalties and clarifications

Umpire

These guys may not be the stars of the show, but they are just as important. Typically, you will find them stationed opposite the ref in the offensive backfield. They will stand around 15 yards deep and position themselves outside the tight end position.

Responsibilities

- counts the number of offensive players to ensure the correct amount is on the field
- monitors the line of scrimmage to look for any potential penalties, such as illegal blocks or holding
- watch out for any illegal players positioned downfield
- watches the quarterback for any passes that go beyond the line of scrimmage
- keeps track of scoring, the number of timeouts used, and how many are left

Down Judge

The down judge, also known as the head linesman, is positioned along the sideline at the line of scrimmage opposite the side of the line judge.

Responsibilities

- monitors the line of scrimmage
- observe closely for any potential encroachment or offside penalties
- calls for out-of-bounds on the sideline
- marks the forward progress of the football and informs the referee of the current down
- keeps track of all eligible receivers
- manages the ball position and is in charge of the chain crew

Line Judge

The line judge will cover the opposite sideline of the down judge; their job may be simple, but they can make decisions that can change the outcome of a game.

Responsibilities

- calls for out-of-bounds on their respective sidelines
- assists the down coach in calling for offside, false starts, and any other calls relating to the line of scrimmage
- acts as the backup timekeeper if needed

Field Judge

Field judges are positioned deep down the field and are stationed behind the secondary on the same side as the line judge.

Responsibilities

- counts the number of defensive players to ensure the correct amount is on the field
- will rule against any pass interferences or holding violations downfield
- makes the call for delay of game penalties
- determines completed passes

Side Judge

The side judge has the same responsibilities as the field judge; however, they will be on the opposite side of the field judge but still deep down in the field.

Back Judge

These guys are the final pair of eyes monitoring and officiating the game. They cover the area of the field between the field judge and the line judge, behind the secondary in the middle of the field.

Responsibilities

- counts the number of defensive players to ensure the correct amount is on the field
- will rule against any passing interference or holding violations that happen downfield in the area between the side and field judges
- rules on pass interference or holding downfield in the area between the side and field judges
- calls delay of game penalties
- will determine completed passes
- rules on whether field goals were successfully made

* * *

Good hustle team, we have covered the rules of football, but now we explore the plays and strategies that make football such a dynamic and exciting sport!

CHAPTER 6

Plays and Game Strategy

I n 1960, San Francisco 49ers coach Red Hickey made football history when he innovated a strategy that incorporated punts, spread passing, and double-wing formations into a formation known as the shotgun. Hickey coined it the shotgun as it sprayed receivers across the field (New England Patriots, 2006).

COMMON OFFENSIVE FORMATIONS

Okay, team, huddle up. It's time to go over some offensive formations and learn the basic offensive strategies that turn up the heat on defenses, put points on the board, and win us games!

Take note of these common offensive formations:

- **Single back formation (AKA the Ace formation):** The quarterback will line up just behind the center, and one running back will feature behind the quarterback. The single-back formation is flexible as it will either feature four wide receivers or three wide receivers and a tight end; therefore, it is effective for both passing and running plays.

- **I formation:** In this formation, there will be two running backs behind the quarterback, and the quarterback will be positioned just behind the center. The fullback will be directly behind the quarterback and the tailback will be directly behind the fullback. Typically, the fullback would run through the hole first to block the linebackers, while the fullback would run through the hole with the football.

- **Shotgun:** The quarterback will be positioned about five to seven feet behind the center. The center will then snap the football through the air to the quarterback. This formation allows the quarterback to have a clearer view of the field and the defense, which enhances opportunities to make effective passes. The only downside is that it limits running plays and generally lets the other team know that a passing play is about to commence.

- **Wildcat:** The wildcat formation features a running back taking the position of a quarterback. Due to the quarterback being absent in the backfield, the focus shifts to running plays, and teams will utilize an extra blocker for the ball carrier. Like the shotgun, this formation often signals what type of play will happen.

- **Pistol:** Similar to the shotgun formation but not quite the same, is the Pistol formation. The quarterback will stand at a shorter distance behind the center but not directly behind him either. This formation provides flexibility and balance as both running and passing plays can be executed as the quarterback maintains closer proximity to the line of scrimmage compared to the shotgun.

COMMON DEFENSIVE FORMATIONS

Alright so we've covered the basic offensive formations, but what about the basic defensive football formations? The defense can win games. These are the most common defensive formations you will find in a football game:

- **4-3 defense:** The 4-3 is made up of four defensive linemen and three linebackers, in addition to two cornerbacks and two safeties. It is renowned for its versatility, as cornerbacks can easily switch with linebackers in passing situations. The superstars of this formation are the defensive ends, as they lead outside pass-rushing attacks and generally produce the most sacks. The D-line is a crucial component of this formation and makes defensive linemen highly sought-after during the draft.
- **3-4 defense:** Similar to the 4-3 formation, however, the 3-4 formation replaces one defensive lineman with a linebacker. Therefore, this formation consists of three linemen, four linebackers, two cornerbacks, and two safeties. The 3-4 formation relies on the speed of the linebacker to provide crucial run coverage and pass rushes. It is also

important to note that the nose tackle needs considerable size to handle multiple offensive linemen, while outside linebackers with both size and speed on their side are extremely sought after for this formation.

- **4-4 defense**: This is a great formation to defend against running plays, as it deploys four linemen and four linebackers, thus packing eight defenders in the box. While this brick wall of defenders is highly effective against running plays, it is vulnerable to passing plays.

- **5-2 defense:** The 5-2 formation is also used to defend against the running game, deploying five linemen and two linebackers to defend. It is generally utilized when defending against a team known for their running plays.

- **6-2 defense:** The 6-2 formation is used for short-yardage situations and is designed to stop the running game. Six defensive linemen are used to cover the gaps between the offensive linemen, while two linebackers are deployed to defend against runs. Cornerbacks and safeties are positioned close to the line to provide defense against passes; however, they still need to execute deep-third responsibilities.

- **5-3 defense:** Once again, this formation is used to defend against running plays by utilizing five linemen and three linebackers. Keep in mind that this formation's linebacker alignment and coverage assignments vary depending on the defensive scheme and game situation. For example, linebackers may be responsible for filling gaps to nullify inside runs while also being mindful to cover potential passing opportunities for running backs and tight ends.

- **Goal line defense:** The middle two linebackers will stay back to stop the running back as they approach the goal line, while the other two linebackers will focus on containment responsibilities. The other six down linemen aim to penetrate the offensive line. If the offense passes, then the two middle linebackers (the ones who remained back) will need to drop back to cover the end zone, while the safety is responsible for watching the quarterback's eyes to read the pass.

SPECIAL TEAM PLAYS

Now that we've got our offense and defense covered let's talk about our special team plays. These plays are reserved for the special team and can be the decisive difference between victory and defeat. These are the most common special team plays you are most likely to see on a football field:

- **Kickoff returns:** This play occurs once the receiving team catches the football after the opposing team kicks off. The objective is simple: Once the returner catches the football, it is their job to shimmy through the opposing coverage team and gain as much yardage as possible. The kickoff return is generally the starting point of a team's offensive possession and is what sets the stage for their team to drive downfield to score crucial points.
- **Punt returns:** This is when the offensive team decides to punt the football and typically happens on

their fourth down when they choose to avoid a field goal attempt or go for a first down. This play is vital to push the opposing team downfield, as they will punt the ball as far down the field as possible. The punt returner will then catch the ball safely and avoid turnovers. They will need quick decision-making to decide whether to run, change direction, or signal for a fair catch. If they run, then their teammates will block to create space for them and protect them from oncoming tacklers. Punt returns can seriously sway the momentum of the game as they provide their team with a favorable field position for the next play.

- **Onside kicks:** These specialized kicks are used by the kicking team to quickly regain possession of the ball. They are generally short, lower kicks that are intended to make it easier for the kicking team to recover the ball once it travels past at least ten yards. These tricky kicks are typically used when a team is behind and time is quickly running out. This is because, in these situations, teams need to regain possession swiftly to pull off an epic comeback. This kick hinges on the kicker's precise execution and timing, in addition to catching the opposing team off guard.

- **Fake punts:** This sly kick is about the element of surprise and is when a punting team lines up in their standard punting formation but tricks the opposition by executing a different play altogether. For instance, the punter could either pass or run with the ball, or they could be extra tricky by utilizing a cheeky direct snap to one of their teammates. The aim is to fool the opposition and extend the offensive possession by going for a first down instead of a kick. Fake punts require careful planning and on-the-mark timing.

- **Trick plays:** The king of deceptive plays are trick plays, which encompass a variety of unconventional tactics and maneuvers to confuse the defense. Whether it be unexpected passes, lateral movements, handoffs, or even utilizing multiple players to pull off silky smooth movements, these plays often leave defenses scratching their heads, or, should I say, helmets. Trick plays have fooled even the most seasoned of defenders. Its primary aim is to deceive the defensive line and exploit their vulnerabilities from that confusion to generate scoring opportunities, gain serious yardage, and rack up points. These plays need to be used sparingly, as you always need to keep the defense guessing.

OFFENSIVE STRATEGIES AND TACTICS

Just as football teams will choose to utilize specific offensive formations, they will also incorporate an array of offensive strategies that are unique to their team's playing styles. Some teams choose to place a significant amount of emphasis on their running game; teams like the Baltimore Ravens, Chicago Bears, and San Francisco 49ers are known for their running game in recent NFL seasons (Fox Sports, 2024). For the running games, you've got the big, burly guys on the offense who excel at opening up running lanes for their agile and speedy running backs to rack up invaluable yardage. Let's not forget the tight ends and even receivers chipping in with solid blocks as well. Teams with formidable running plays are adept at grinding out yards, giving their defenses a break to rest, and are experts at controlling the clock.

While the running game is great, it doesn't always get teams those big-yard gains that get their team downfield fast. Some of the most prevalent pass-happy teams in recent years include the Dallas Cowboys, Miami Dolphins, and Philadelphia Eagles (NFL, 2024). Teams that excel at passing need an offensive line that is quick on their feet and adept at protecting their quarterbacks. It is up to the tight ends, running backs, and receivers to make sure they make those crucial catches. These teams are incredibly exciting and don't waste time lighting up the scoreboard; however, they are also more prone to turnovers due to how much time the ball spends in the air.

While running and passing make up the majority of an offensive strategy, we can't forget about spreading offense. When teams opt for a spread offense, a football game becomes like a chessboard. The offense will spread its players throughout the field, making it difficult for defenses to cover all the offensive players. This leaves openings in the field for the offense to exploit by either using quick passes or cheeky runs downfield.

Finally, we have one of my favorite offense strategies just because of how clever and difficult it is to defend against; this is known as play-action passing. This strategy is like watching a magic trick: the offense will fake a run play, and then bam! They'll trick everybody, even the fans, as the quarterback will launch the football downfield to a receiver while the opposing defense is still trying to figure out what hit them. Play-action passing is generally used sparingly, as offenses always strive to keep the defense guessing.

There's no right or wrong offensive strategy; in fact, a good football team should incorporate a mixture of all of them throughout the game. It is important to note that these offensive strategies take countless hours of training to perfect, and the success of these strategies hinges on effective communication between the coaches and players, studying the opponent's weaknesses, and executing the game plan to perfection.

DEFENSIVE STRATEGIES AND TACTICS

Defending in football is far more than strategic formational lineups; one of the most effective defensive strategies is man-to-man coverage. Essentially, defenders have appointed receivers to cover and stick to them as if they were their shadows. It's no easy feat to pull off, but it's extremely exciting to watch how defenders lock down their assigned targets and how much of a nightmare it is for quarterbacks to find an open man to deliver a pass to.

Then you get situational defensive strategies, like when offenses are near the goal line, forcing defenses to dig deep to prevent the offense from reaching the end zone and scoring. Every inch counts, and one slip-up could cost them their lead or be the reason the gap between the two scores is steadily increasing. When defenses are faced with this hair-raising scenario, they will tighten up their formation and stack the line of scrimmage with defenders to prevent short-yard gains from the offense. Additionally, they will deploy linebackers to fill the gaps, make use of linemen to anchor against the run, and utilize defensive backs to act as support and do everything they can to nullify scoring opportunities.

Next, defenders need to put an end to the passing game; a key defensive strategy to do this is known as a "blitz." Blitz defense consists of using unexpected defenders not typically deployed to rush the quarterback. This unexpected play and increased pressure on the quarterback increase the likelihood of a sack and disruption to a quarterback's timing. The only downside is that it leaves few defensive players downfield to cover runners and receivers.

Lastly, football teams can use a defensive strategy known as "prevent defense." This strategy is typically used late in games when a team adds an extra defensive back and positions defenders behind receivers. Prevent defense helps to defend against long passes, forcing offenses to use short passes or runs. Therefore, prevent defense limits the opportunities for the offense to make big plays and preserves the lead of the defending team.

The offense might get points on the board, but a solid defense has won countless games for their teams. There's nothing quite like watching a defense shut down an offensive lineup play after play.

GAME MANAGEMENT AND CLOCK CONTROL

Effective game management and controlling the clock are essential strategic aspects in football, especially for coaches, as they provide teams with an upper hand to secure victory. Clock management, strategic timeouts, and expert strategic decisions can all enhance a team's chances of victory.

Clock Management

Clock management is all about a team's ability to strategically use time to their advantage. It's about finding the perfect balance between running down the clock and scoring valuable points, especially when the game is nearing its end and the scores are close. Teams often run down the clock by running with the ball to keep the clock ticking, making short, quick passes with high success rates to move the ball forward, and using timeouts wisely to control the momentum of the game. In these situations, time is a football team's best friend.

Timeouts Usage

In football games, each team is given three timeouts that last up to two minutes each. Teams use these timeouts for a variety of reasons, but most commonly to control the game clock, regroup, strategize, and help players stay focused. A timeout can be called by the coach or any player. To signal a timeout, players will form a "T" shape with their hands.

Strategic timeouts can drastically influence a game; they can conserve time and prevent crucial mistakes by giving players time to get their rhythm back and disrupt the opposing team's momentum. Coaches and players consider several factors before calling a timeout, such as the situation of the game, the score, and the remaining time. Take note that while each team gets three timeouts per half, unused timeouts will not be carried over to the second half. Additionally, timeouts are not allowed to be used consecutively on the same scrimmage down.

Here are some common time-out strategies:

- Using an early timeout to disrupt the opposition's momentum after they made a big play or put early points on the board. This allows players to regroup and regain their rhythm.
- Keeping at least one timeout per half reserved for any unexpected late-half/late-game drama. This allows teams to strategically realign in high-tension moments in the game.
- Calling a timeout if the game clock is running down, the offensive seems disorganized, and to prevent your team from running the risk of a delay of game penalty.
- Calling a timeout before the snap as the coach notices their defense looks confused or misaligned allows the defense to realign correctly and avoid potential mistakes.
- Using a timeout to break an opposing kicker's concentration just before a vital field goal attempt. This will add increased pressure on the kicker and make it harder for them to make the field goal.
- Making use of a timeout if the offense is looking shaky, thus preventing costly turnovers or tackles which would result in a heavy loss of yardage.
- Utilizing a timeout to instruct players to set up practiced plays such as a Hail Mary just before the half or game ends.
- Burning through a team's remaining timeouts to stop the clock, manipulate the momentum, and prevent unnecessary scoring.

Decision-Making in Critical Situations

Great decision-making can win games, and indecisiveness can just as easily lose a game for their team. In crucial situations such as two-minute drills (an offensive series of plays to score points quickly near the end of a half or game) or defending your goal line in the final moments of a game, these situations require razor-sharp decision-making and meticulous planning to turn the tables and lead a team to victory. Thus, coaches are thrown into the spotlight and are forced to make split-second decisions regarding which plays to call, clock management, and how to best utilize their players.

In these high-stakes moments, successful decision-making hinges on a coach's ability to delicately balance acute situational awareness, strategic foresight, and unwavering confidence in the team's ability during high-pressure situations. It is up to the coach to anticipate what the opponent's next move will be, in addition to leveraging his team's strengths to exploit the opposition's weaknesses.

For instance, if a team were to run a two-minute drill, the coach would orchestrate a quick yet highly methodical offensive drive by balancing quick snappy plays in conjunction with the preservation of timeouts. If the coach's team is defending the goal line in the final moments of the game, then he would need to deploy the perfect combination of defenders in a goal-line defensive formation to thwart the opposing offense's advances.

In these high-tension moments, the players may be the ones on the field, but the coach is the one pulling the strings with their bold yet calculated decisions.

* * *

Now that we've comprehensively studied our playbook and the different strategies on a football field, it's game time! We'll explore all the tips and tricks to enjoy your very first game day.

CHAPTER 7

Your Game Day Guide

NFL season tickets are difficult to get your hands on, to say the least, but there's one NFL team with such an insanely long waiting list that it is almost too unbelievable to believe. With approximately 137,000 people on the waiting list and only around 700 pairs of season tickets to go around each season, the wait for Green Bay Packers tickets stretches for centuries. If these tickets weren't scarce enough for you, these tickets are transferable, meaning they get passed down to family generations, never returning to the overall pool of tickets. Taking that into consideration, it is believed a fan can wait up to 1,000 years to get their hands on one of these highly sought-after season tickets (The Wander Club, 2022)!

PREGAME PREPARATION: GETTING READY FOR KICKOFF

It's game time! Let's see those game faces! A football game begins before a ball is even kicked or thrown. There are long-standing traditions, rituals, and unique ways teams and fans get hyped before the big kickoff. From tailgating to team traditions, from navigating the stadium to player quirks to get them amped before a game, we'll be covering them all!

Tailgating

A football game just wouldn't be a football game without a sea of fans hyping themselves up outside of the stadium before a big game. To countries outside of America, tailgating may mean driving too close to another vehicle, while to others, it may mean when you drop down your pickup truck to load it with furniture and other big items. However, to Americans, tailgating is a lifestyle!

That's right, tailgating is far more than simply loading a cooler full of food in your car and heading to the stadium—it is a cherished cultural tradition in the land of the free for football fans. Just imagine, for a moment, a parking lot flooded with fans transforming a mundane location into a pregame party frenzy before kickoff. It's truly a scene to behold; tailgating is all about wholesome comradery, grilled foot, and plenty to drink. The history of tailgating is a little fuzzy; some say it can be traced back to ancient harvest festivals, while others believe it was started by the French eating their hearts out by the guillotine. Regardless of its origin, one thing's for sure: It's about community, fans bonding with other fans, and a whole lot of food and beverages.

Today, tailgating is an integral part of the Football experience. Fans gather, bringing their own barbecue grills, coolers filled with drinks, and signature dishes from their region. In the South, it's barbecue and slaw, while in Louisiana, it's gumbo. Midwest fans love their brats (sausages), and in New England, clam chowder is a staple.

So, before the game begins, immerse yourself in the tailgate culture. It's more than just a pregame ritual—it's a celebration of football, friends, and the American spirit.

Stadium Etiquette

Attending a live football game, especially the Super Bowl, is incredibly exciting. Our emotions run wild, and we tend to get caught up in the moment. This is all fine and dandy, and in fact, it is encouraged. I mean, this is football we are talking about, baby! However, we need to be respectable and follow some basic stadium etiquette to ensure it is an enjoyable experience for everyone. Following stadium etiquette includes:

- **Respect seating norms.** Try to choose a section in the stadium where both sitting and standing are customary; typically, this is found at the end zone (Vult, 2015). However, be mindful not to obstruct another fan's view by standing in front of them excessively, especially if you find the majority of the crowd is sitting. Keep in mind standing is generally accepted if your team scores points through a field goal, touchdown, or any other method.
- **Familiarize yourself with prohibited items.** Obviously, items such as firearms, fireworks, knives, and other commonly prohibited items are not allowed in the stadium. Think of it as if you were entering an airport. Additionally, altered helmets, hats with spikes, or clothing that will obstruct the views of other fans are not allowed. Alcohol is not permitted to be brought into the premises but can be bought once you are in the stadium; however, stadium alcohol is pretty pricey, so if you are looking for a buzz, tailgating is your best bet (Ford Field, 2023).
- **Be mindful of your bag size.** The NFL has a limit on the size of bag permitted to be brought inside a

stadium; furthermore, your bag will be checked at the gate. Backpacks, duffel bags, diaper bags, packages, briefcases, gym bags, and fanny packs will not be allowed inside the stadium (Commanders, 2023).

- **Watch your language.** Remember that football games have children spectators, and, therefore, the NFL and fans pride themselves on creating a family-friendly environment at games, so avoid using foul language.
- **Be a good sport.** Good sportsmanship is a must. Don't start fights, treat fellow fans respectfully, don't throw anything, cuss, or throw racial slurs at the players, and treat the stadium staff with courtesy.
- **Exhibit team spirit.** Wear your team colors proudly, but remember to take your cap off and stand while the national anthem is being sung.

Iconic NFL Team Traditions

While many celebrations and traditions are upheld nationwide in the NFL, some teams have their own unique celebrations and customs that they pride themselves on when rooting for their beloved teams. These are some of the most iconic fan-and-player-led NFL team traditions.

Terrible Towel

If we are talking about iconic team traditions, none is more legendary than the terrible towel. This tradition is the symbol of the Pittsburgh Steelers's fandom. The terrible towel can be traced back to 1975, when Myron Cope, a beloved Pittsburgh sports broadcaster, introduced it as a way to rally the morale of the Steelers. You may be thinking it's just a towel, right? Well, it's way more than that—it embodies the unwavering support and pride of Steelers fans.

Its significance has extended beyond the field and has even brought heartwarming stories such as comforting Steeler fans battling cancer as well as being waved proudly in the air during life milestones. The terrible towel has served as the link between the Steelers and their supporters for generations, symbolizing the deep emotional connection between the highs and lows of Pittsburgh football (Gridiron Sport, 2023).

Minnesota Vikings "SKOL!"

Skol is a term that is rooted in Scandinavian history and is derived from Old Norse, meaning "cheers." Seeing that the Vikings are the symbol of the Minnesota football franchise, it seems fitting, right? "Skol" serves as a rallying cry for Viking fans and never fails to ignite their team and fans to up a gear.

When Minnesota Viking fans unite, they chant "Skol Vikings!" followed by a rhythmic clap that engulfs the stadiums. This creates an atmosphere buzzing with unity and unwavering support. This chant is executed throughout the game, whether it be player introductions to crucial moments in the game or for key tackles, and it never fails to bring the stadium to life (Gridiron Sport, 2023)!

Atlanta Dirty Bird

The Atlanta "Dirty Bird" dance can be traced back to when Jamal Anderson, a running back for the Atlanta Falcons, celebrated a touchdown with an iconic dance that later got the name "Dirty Bird." Anderson's celebratory dance not only symbolized victory but also exuberated and united his team and the fanbase. Since then, fans and players often replicate this dance during touchdowns, and it has become a staple during Falcon games. This iconic fan tradition has rooted itself deeply in the hearts of Atlanta football fans (Gridiron Sport, 2023).

Buffalo Bills Table Smash

Since around 2015, Buffalo Bills fans have seen die-hard fans leaping through folding tables as they wear their team colors with pride. This may seem extreme from an outsider's perspective but to a Bills fan, the table smash is a spirited display of passion and devotion to their team. This bizarre tradition has become a staple these days, but that doesn't mean it doesn't come with risks. So be mindful to approach the table smash with an air of caution (Allegiant Goods Co, 2022).

THE PROCEDURE BEFORE KICKOFF

So, we've had our fun at the tailgate, but now kickoff is fast approaching. What does this mean for teams and players alike? Well, it means that both teams will meticulously prepare 12 primary and 12 backup Wilson official NFL footballs; each one of these balls needs to meet the strict standards of the NFL. These balls will be given to the referee for inspection (NFL Football Operations, 2024a).

Next on the list is a 60-minute medical meeting that happens one hour before kickoff and ensures players are match-fit and emphasizes player safety. Additionally, players will undergo last-minute pregame treatment, which will range from massages to stem therapy, to ensure they are in optimal condition for the game (NFL, 2022).

Lastly, players will step onto the field to familiarize themselves with the stadium and the playing surface so they can strategize how they can best navigate the field come game time. Alright, everything seems in order—it's game time, baby!

PLAYER PREGAME RITUALS

Pregame preparation for a game isn't just for the fans; many players have adopted a variety of unique and often bizarre pregame rituals. These are some of the best of the bunch (Riddler, 2012).

John Henderson's Wake-Up Slap

Jacksonville Jaguars defensive tackle John Henderson had a rather unique pregame ritual before game time. His ritual of choice is to get slapped hard right across his face by one of the members of the training staff. I'm sure you're wondering why. It's simple: Henderson believed this slap will alleviate all of his pregame jitters and get him pumped up for the game ahead (Riddle, 2012).

Brian Urlacher's Cookie Obsession

Legendary linebacker Brian Urlacher had a less intense pregame ritual than Henderson; however, it was still pretty bizarre. Before a game, he always ate exactly two chocolate chip cookies, and yes, before you ask, it had to be two, no less and no more. What is the reason behind this? Who knows, but it worked; the man was a monster on the field (Riddle, 2012).

Sam Bradford's Three-Food Rule

St. Louis Rams's Sam Bradford had another food-related pregame ritual but it was even more head-scratching than Brian Urlacher's. Bradford has a strict rule that he has to eat everything in sets of three. Whether it was cantaloupe, pineapple, or any other food, it needed to be in a set of three to bring him luck (Riddle, 2012).

Jermichael Finley's Pregame Pedicure

Who said athletes can't take time for a little self-care? Well, Green Bay Packers quarterback Jermichael Finley was a big advocate for looking after one's nails; in fact, he would make sure to get a pedicure just hours before he played a Monday night football game. This odd pregame ritual was Finley's way of pampering himself and ensuring he was game-ready from head to toe, but that begs the question: Why only on a Monday (Riddle, 2012)?

UNDERSTANDING THE BROADCAST

Watching a live football game is an incredible experience; however, it isn't always possible. The next best option is to watch the game live on TV, but first, we need to familiarize ourselves with the various NFL broadcast elements to enhance our viewing experience.

First off, we have the commentary. Commentary is crucial for TV viewing as it serves to keep viewers informed about the unfolding match. Traditionally, a solo commentator used to lead the narrative, but in modern times, football games now feature co-commentators. Co-commentating adds some spice to our viewing pleasure and often consists of former players who provide their diverse perspectives on the game (By Association, 2017).

The quality of NFL commentating is fantastic, and each commentator meticulously prepares notes filled with stats, records, and historical references to enrich the commentary and aid in adding depth to current and past NFL action. If you're still new to football, then don't hesitate to use the glossary in this guide. The glossary aids in comprehending commentators' remarks so you can have an even better viewing experience.

Additionally, for those of you who are still getting the hang of football, understanding the broadcast graphics is crucial, as these graphics aid viewers in understanding key aspects of the game. Take note of the various graphics commonly seen during televised football games:

- **Possession:** The possession graphic indicates which team currently has possession of the football. For instance, the graphic will show "Team A (e.g., Baltimore Ravens)" or "Team B (e.g., New England Patriots)." If one of these teams is shown, it means that the team is controlling the ball at that moment.
- **Score:** This will show the current score in the game. It will showcase the points that each team has scored, for instance, "Kansas City Chiefs: 21" and "Cincinnati Bengals: 14."
- **Timeouts remaining:** This graphic will show the number of timeouts that each team has remaining. For example: "Miami Dolphins: 3 timeouts remaining" and "St. Louis Rams: 1 timeout remaining."

- **Quarter:** This indicates which quarter of the game is currently being played. It will indicate either "1st Quarter," "2nd Quarter," "3rd Quarter," or "4th Quarter" based on how much time has been played.
- **Time left in the quarter:** In addition to showing what quarter is being played, the broadcast will also indicate how much time is left to be played in the current quarter. For instance, if the graphic displays "9:42," it means there are 9 minutes and 42 seconds remaining in that quarter.
- **Down and distance:** This will show which down a team is currently sitting on and how many yards (distance) the offense needs to advance for a first down. For example, if the graphic indicates "2nd and 2," it means that a team is on their 2nd down and only needs to make 2 yards for a first down.
- **Play time left on the clock:** This indicates how much time is left for the overall game to be played. This helps fans viewing the broadcast track the time available for each team to make plays and potentially score.

Once you get the hang of all these graphics and the lingo the commentators add to the game, your viewing experience will be far more immersive, and you will gain a richer understanding of these wonderful sports dynamics.

KEY STATISTICS TO BE AWARE OF

Football is a numbers game, so keeping that in mind, stats are extremely important and tell an entire story of their own.

Keeping tabs on stats can provide fans with valuable insights into how their team is performing. These are some of the most crucial team stats to keep an eye on:

Yardage

Points look great on the board, but without valuable yardage being made, there would be no points. Yardage stats provide fans with crucial insights into how well our team is doing. Key yardage stats to look out for include offensive yards per carry, offensive yards per attempt, and offensive starting positions. Offensive yards per carry mean how many yards were made per rushing attempt; offensive yards per attempt indicate the average yards of an attempted pass; and offensive starting positions highlight the location on the field where an offensive team begins their possession of the ball. These yardage indicators help us assess our team's scoring potential and offensive efficiency.

Defensive Points Allowed Per 100 Yards

These are extremely informative stats, as they help us gauge our team's defensive performance based on how many points are awarded to opposing offenses per 100 yards. We can determine this stat by adding the total yards our teams have given away, dividing them by 100, and then dividing that by the points scored against our team. This will determine a team's defensive effectiveness. Take note that a consistent result below six showcases a strong defensive performance.

Turnover Margin

Turnovers are like striking gold in a football game and can often decide a game; therefore, turnover margin statistics are key to consider when analyzing our team's performance. Some may say turnovers are reliant on luck, while others may say a player can read a game. Regardless of which one is true, analyzing turnover margins can help identify a team's strengths and weaknesses.

Time on Possession

Possession wins games, simple as that. Time on possession is a stat that indicates how much control a team has over the game. High stats of time on possession indicate offensive dominance and defensive rest. Not only that, but it also demonstrates a team's ability to manage a game and correlates with the overall team performance. I mean, you can't score points if you don't have the ball, right?

Point Differential

Rather than looking at a team's win-loss record, analyzing a team's point differential is a more accurate metric to predict their future success. Simply put, this is when you take the total points a team has scored in the season and subtract it from the number of points they have given away. If a team boasts a positive point differential, then wins tend to follow, and the opposite is true for a negative point differential.

Now that we're all prepped for game day let's take a little trip down memory lane to appreciate some of the most iconic plays, strategies, and moments to ever grace a football field.

CHAPTER 8

Iconic Plays and Game-Changing Moments

Have you ever wondered what the longest field goal in NFL history was? Well, that record is held by Baltimore Ravens kicker Justin Tucker, who made an incredible 66-yard field goal in 2021 (Oliver, 2024).

UNSTOPPABLE PLAYS

The NFL has witnessed some magical plays over its illustrious history, but some stand out more than others. When we think of game-winning plays, these masterful plays come to mind.

The New England Patriots Red-Zone "ISO" Slant to Gronkowski (Between 2010–2018)

Back when Rob Gronkowski and Tom Brady were playing together for the New England Patriots between 2010 and 2018, they had a play that gave opposing defenses nightmares and for good reason. New England would leverage Rob Gronkowski's strengths by tactically removing him from the tight end position and re-aligning him as a receiver by running a slant route toward the middle of the field.

This strategy would force the opposing team to make defensive adjustments and would strong-arm defenses to make their linebackers, safeties, and often their cornerbacks cover Gronkowski; however, Ron Gronkowski's size, power, and athleticism often made this an extremely difficult task.

As I said, Gronkowski would now act as an additional receiver, particularly in the "red zone" (between the 20-yard line and the goal line), which would cause havoc for defenses as they would often be mismatched, resulting in easy scoring opportunities for the Patriots.

One effective formation used by the Patriots is known as the "Dakota" alignment. This is a 3 x 1 formation, which essentially means there will be three eligible receivers lined up on one side of the field and one eligible receiver on the other side. In this formation, Gronkowski would act as the isolated backside receiver. This formation was deadly as it provided clear one-on-one matches for Tom Brady, the Patriots quarterback, to exploit.

It was Gronkowski's expert skill at establishing leverage inside on slant routes as he shielded defenders and created separation to receive passes from Brady that made this play virtually unstoppable. Rob Gronkowski's dominance on the field in creating favorable matchups helped his team consistently capitalize on scoring plays efficiently, making defenses shake in their cleats trying to contain the impact of this game-winning play (Bowen, 2018)!

The Cowboys' Back-Shoulder Fade to Dez Bryant (Between 2010–2016)

This play was deadly for any defensive lineup to deal with between 2010 and 2016 when wide receiver Dez Bryant and quarterback Tony Romo were making mincemeat of defenders for the Dallas Cowboys. For this play, wide receiver Dez Bryant and quarterback Tony Romo ran the show. This play was primarily used inside the red zone, where the Dallas Cowboys would leverage Tony Romo's precision passing and Dez Bryant's seemingly unstoppable back-shoulder fade catches. A back-shoulder fade is a type of pass in football where the receiver runs along the sidelines toward the end zone, and the quarterback throws the football toward the receiver's back shoulder to create space for the defender.

The Cowboys would use this play to capitalize on Dez Bryant's incredible combination of ball skills, body control, leaping ability, and strength. These true athletic qualities allowed Bryant to force mismatches with the defense and create separation from them in tight spaces. However, for this play to work, the timing and placement of Tony Romo's passes were essential. Romo needed to ensure pinpoint accuracy when he threw the ball behind Bryant's back shoulder. It was up to Romo's delivery skills to give Bryant a realistic chance of making the catch.

The position of the throw neutralizes the opposing defender's leverage and maximizes Bryant's talent of adjusting his body to the ball mid-flight to make unbelievable receptions and big gains for the Dallas Cowboys. This play truly showcased Bryant's exceptional body control and ball-tracking skills.

Ultimately, the back-shoulder fade allowed Bryant to exploit the backs' vulnerability and make contested catches in tight coverage; it's no easy feat and not something just any player could pull off. However, thanks to Bryant's superhuman ability to win one-on-one battles in sticky situations and Romo's precision passing, the combination was almost unstoppable (Bowen, 2018).

The Packers's "Sting" Route to Jordy Nelson (Between 2008–2018)

The "sting" route fooled many defensive players when Jordy Nelson and Aaron Rodgers were linking up for the Packers between 2008 and 2018. In this play, the Green Bay Packers made use of a deadly shot play known as the "sting" route, which was an essential strategy in their overall offensive game. It was designed to allow them to use play action (a play that appears to be a running play but turns out to be a passing play) as well as execute an eight-man protection to throw a shot straight over the top of the defense.

This unstoppable play was made possible by wide receiver Jordy Nelson, who executed a deep double move. He would initially deceive the defense with a corner route and then quickly break back to the post, which would create a separation in the defense for quarterback Aaron Rodgers to exploit with a killer pass. This route placed an obscene amount of pressure on the opposing team's deep-half safety, which forced the defense to maintain their position against Nelson's lightning-speed run downfield.

The key to the success of this play was Nelson's ability to fool the defense with his double move without exposing his intentions. To finish off this bamboozling run, Nelson was aided by the Packers' pre-snap alignment and play action. With Nelson often positioned in a reduced split (when the receiver is positioned close to the core of the formation), it created a closed-side play action from the Packers, allowing Aaron Rodgers plenty of time to survey the field as Nelson accelerated downfield for a receive. This clever play meant that there would be a one-on-one matchup with the opposing safety, allowing Nelson's adept route running to expose the defense's poor technique or over-commitment.

This play made even the best safeties in the NFL struggle. In a game against the Minnesota Vikings, Nelson flawlessly executed the "sting" route, forcing safety Harrison Smith to lose his leverage by tricking him with his converted double move, leaving him vulnerable to Rodgers' downfield strike. However, Harrison Smith wasn't the only victim of Nelson's exceptional running; Nelson would often use his speed and route-running savvy to create gaps in the defense to make valuable big gains and touchdowns and was an integral player in the Packers offense and the superstar of the sting route (Bowen, 2018)!

Steelers' Counter-Offensive With Le'Veon Bell (Between 2013–2015)

In the modern NFL, the passing game dominates. However, the Pittsburgh Steelers had a powerful running play, known as the counter-offense, back when Le'Veon Bell, David DeCastro, and Heath Miller were terrorizing defenders for the Steelers between 2013 and 2015.

This play was designed to capitalize on the vision, balance, and speedy acceleration of running back Le'Veon Bell. While this play may not be as flashy as the others, it is just as menacing and difficult to deal with for opposing defenses. The counter offense relied on a counter action (a running play that begins in one direction but ends in a different direction) in the backfield and the ability to pull blockers play side.

What set Pittsburgh apart was how they could expertly make use of their personnel and alignment to attack the defense's edge, which created running lanes for Bell to exploit. This was achieved by withering one or two back sets; the play used the backside guard as well as the halfback to pull blockers sideways. This allowed the Steelers to dictate the opposing blocking scheme and force the cornerback to set the edge.

Bell needed to be disciplined, and his ability to remain patient was vital. If he ran too early before the blockers opened routes for him, he would have been taken down. Guard David DeCastro and tight end Heath Miller often created favorable blocking matchups to create the running lanes for Bell to exploit. The alignment of this play forced the cornerback to contend with DeCastro, which was more often than not a mismatch, giving Bell lanes to run through. This provided Pittsburgh with a strategic advantage, as this play often forced the cornerback to widen or retreat as they were unable to handle DeCastro's pull to the edge.

It may not have been the flashiest play around, but add Bell's running skills, DeCastro's athleticism, and Miller's blocking prowess, and defenses were looking at one of the most troublesome plays in the NFL to defend against (Bowen, 2018).

GAME-CHANGING MOMENTS

You've got to love football—it's given us so many legendary moments that have kept the fans talking for years. Some go back decades but remain etched in the brains of football fans generations later. While countless iconic moments have taken place on a football field, these are the five that stand out.

The Immaculate Reception

Possibly one of the most iconic moments ever to happen on a football field happened way back in 1972 during an AFC match between the Oakland Raiders and Pittsburgh Steelers. So, what makes this game-changing moment so iconic? Well, here's what happened: Pittsburgh Steelers quarterback Terry Bradshaw was faced with immense pressure from the Raider's defense, but Bradshaw never let this phase him; instead of getting overwhelmed by the chaos unfolding in front of him, he pulled off a rocket of a pass downfield.

Bradshaw's pass ricocheted off a collision between Steelers' receiver John "Frenchy" Fuqua and Raiders safety Jack Tatum. As you can imagine, the deflection was met with drama and pandemonium; however, hope was not lost as running back Franco Harris miraculously caught the ball in stride and sprinted toward the end zone to score a game-winning touchdown.

For over 50 years, this catch has been etched in the memories of football fans and has since been coined as the "Immaculate Reception." This play got its name from Pittsburgh sportscaster Myron Cope, and it truly encapsulates the unbelievable nature of this play. Despite the Steelers losing in the playoffs that year, the immaculate reception is often considered the catalyst for the Steelers football dynasty in the 1970s. To this day, it is considered one of the most iconic moments in NFL history (NFL, 2019).

Justin Tucker's Mammoth Kick

This field goal in 2021 etched the name of Justin Tucker in the NFL history books. Tucker's 66-yard field goal was almost like watching a football movie play out. Time was running out; the Ravens were down 16–17 to the Detroit Lions, and this kick would decide it all. Add the fact that it is the longest field goal ever made in the NFL, and you've got yourself one hell of a movie-like scenario.

Well, he broke the record and won the game for the Ravens. Tucker wasn't one to miss many kicks, to begin with, but his 66-yard field goal is what he will always be remembered for. Tucker was having the season of his life before this field goal; he had already made an impressive 49 consecutive field goals leading up to the record-breaking kick. Even with those numbers, even the most optimistic of fans were surely doubting his ability to pull off the impossible (Oliver, 2024). It just goes to show: Never write off the impossible!

The Catch

Two words are all that's needed for every football fan to know exactly what you're talking about, and they are "The Catch." Arguably the most iconic moment in football. The catch happened in 1982, when the San Francisco 49ers found themselves facing defeat in the face against the Dallas Cowboys in the NFC Championship game. There were less than five minutes left on the clock when quarterback Joe Montana unleashed a legendary drive from the 11-yard line.

The tension was palpable in the stadium as Montana threw a seemingly hopeless Hail Mary toward the end zone, all while being rushed with immense pressure from the Cowboy's defensive efforts. It seemed like all hope was lost when Receiver Freddie Solomon slipped; however, a miracle happened when Dwight Clark emerged from the back of the end zone to catch Montana's high pass and score the winning touchdown, leading the 49ers to a narrow 28–27 victory.

Clark's seemingly suspended catch in mid-air would forever be known as "The Catch" and the beginning of the 49ers dynasty in the NFL. The catch not only secured the 49ers's first appearance at the Super Bowl but became one of the greatest moments in the NFL (NFL, 2019).

The Helmet Catch

Most wide receivers pride themselves on a great pair of hands, but how many can claim to use their helmet to catch a football? The answer? Not many. However, David Tyree can. It was Super Bowl XLII and the Patriots were on the verge of securing a perfect season, but the New York Giants and Tyree were having none of that.

There were only two minutes of the game remaining and the Patriots were holding on to a slim four-point lead. It wasn't looking good for the Giants; they were facing a critical third-and-five on their 44-yard line. The New Yorkers would need a miracle. Enter the "Helmet Catch!"

In a last-ditch effort, Giants quarterback Eli Manning managed to evade New England's relentless pass rush. Manning was on the verge of being sacked but managed to break free from the onslaught and launch a desperate pass attempt downfield. Then the unbelievable happened: David Tyree soared into the air, battling safety Rodney Harrison for possession. Despite Harrisons' best efforts to dislodge the ball from the wide receiver, Tyree miraculously controlled the football by securing it against his helmet with his right hand before securing it with both. This unbelievable 32-yard reception not only awarded the Giants with much-needed yardage but also ignited the Giants players with the belief that they could win the Super Bowl.

That's exactly what happened; they won the game when Manning connected with Plaxico Burress for the game-winning touchdown. While Tyree never scored the winning touchdown, his insane helmet catch is what inspired his side to win the greatest prize in football (NFL, 2019).

The "Music City Miracle" Touchdown

Back in January 2000, the Tennessee Titans faced off against the Buffalo Bills in the AFC Wild Card game and were dealing with a seemingly insurmountable deficit 16–15 with just 16 seconds remaining. However, the Titans refused to give up that easily, Lorenzo Neal, the Titans fullback, fielded the short kickoff at the 25-yard line and immediately gave the ball to Tennessee's tight end, Frank Wycheck. With an electric burst of speed, Wycheck dashed to his right before skillfully executing a sudden stop and pivot and launching a pinpoint lateral throw across the field to wide receiver Kevin Dyson.

Dyson received the football, found himself with acres of space down the left channel, and was protected by a convoy of blockers to shield him from oncoming defenders. The Bills were left dumbfounded by Tennessee's trickery and were forced to watch Dyson sprint down the field to score the winning touchdown. As you can imagine, the Tennessee fans were left with their jaws hanging to the floor after witnessing the astonishing turn of events, which soon erupted into jubilation.

However, there was still more drama to come; officials reviewed the legality of the lateral pass from Wycheck, which was deemed legal and the Titan fans were buzzing with joy as they watched their side win 22–16. This historic moment propelled the Titans to their first Super Bowl since their days as the Houston Oilers in 1993. This last-minute play would be known as the "Music City Miracle Touchdown" (NFL, 2022a).

* * *

Now that we've covered the legendary plays and iconic moments that have made football the incredibly exciting sport that it is today, there is still one last thing on our agenda. We will explore what teams make up the NFL, their team colors, and their beloved mascots.

CHAPTER 9

Teams, Colors, and Mascots

The NFL is comprised of 32 teams, each with its own unique colors and mascots.

NFL TEAMS

The 32 NFL teams are divided into two divisions: the American Football Conference (AFC) division and the National Football Conference (NFC). Each division has 16 teams.

The AFC Teams

The AFC is further divided into four teams from the north, south, east, and west.

AFC North

- Baltimore Ravens
- Cleveland Browns
- Pittsburgh Steelers
- Cincinnati Bengals

AFC East

- Buffalo Bills
- Miami Dolphins
- New York Jets
- New England Patriots

AFC West

- Kansas City Chiefs
- Las Vegas Raiders
- Denver Broncos
- Los Angeles Chargers

AFC South

- Houston Texans
- Jacksonville Jaguars
- Indianapolis Colts
- Tennessee Titans

The NFC Teams

The NFC is further divided into four teams from the north, south, east, and west.

NFC East

- Dallas Cowboys
- New York Giants
- Philadelphia Eagles
- Washington Commanders

NFC West

- Arizona Cardinals
- Los Angeles Rams
- San Francisco 49ers
- Seattle Seahawks

NFC North

- Chicago Bears
- Detroit Lions
- Green Bay Packers
- Minnesota Vikings

NFC South

- Atlanta Falcons
- Carolina Panthers
- New Orleans Saints
- Tampa Bay Buccaneers

NFL TEAM COLORS

Each NFL team has its own unique color scheme, which is its identity to the fans who support them.

- **Baltimore Ravens:** Purple, black, gold, and red
- **Cleveland Browns:** Brown and orange
- **Pittsburgh Steelers:** Gold, black, blue, red, and silver
- **Cincinnati Bengals:** Orange and black

- **Buffalo Bills:** Blue and red
- **Miami Dolphins:** Aqua, orange, and blue
- **New York Jets:** Green, black, and white
- **New England Patriots:** Nautical blue, red, and silver
- **Kansas City Chiefs:** Red and gold
- **Las Vegas Raiders:** Black and silver
- **Denver Broncos:** Orange and navy
- **Los Angeles Chargers:** Blue, gold, and white
- **Houston Texans:** Steel blue and red
- **Jacksonville Jaguars:** Black, gold, dark gold, and teal
- **Indianapolis Colts:** Blue and gray
- **Tennessee Titans:** Navy, blue, red, and silver
- **Dallas Cowboys:** Royal blue, silver, silver-green, and white
- **New York Giants:** Dark blue, red, and gray
- **Philadelphia Eagles:** Green, black, charcoal, and silver (jersey and helmet)
- **Washington Commanders:** Burgundy and gold
- **Arizona Cardinals:** Red, black, and yellow
- **Los Angeles Rams:** Blue, gold, dark gold, yellow, and white
- **San Francisco 49ers:** Red and gold
- **Seattle Seahawks:** Navy, green, and gray
- **Chicago Bears:** Navy and orange
- **Detroit Lions:** Blue, silver, black, and white
- **Green Bay Packers:** Dark green and gold
- **Minnesota Vikings:** Purple and gold
- **Atlanta Falcons:** Red, black, and silver
- **Carolina Panthers:** Blue, black, and silver

- **New Orleans Saints:** Gold and black
- **Tampa Bay Buccaneers:** Red, orange, black, gray, and pewter

TEAM MASCOTS

No team would be complete without its signature mascot. Welcome to the stage, the iconic NFL mascots.

- **Big Red (Arizona Cardinals):** A large, red cardinal bird with a friendly and energetic demeanor.
- **Freddie Falcon (Atlanta Falcons):** A sleek and athletic falcon with bold feathers and a determined expression.
- **Poe (Baltimore Ravens):** A mystical raven with dark feathers and an intelligent gaze inspired by the famous poet Edgar Allan Poe.
- **Billy Buffalo (Buffalo Bills):** A proud and spirited blue buffalo.
- **Sir Purr (Carolina Panthers):** A playful and mischievous panther with sleek black fur and bright green eyes.
- **Staley Da Bear (Chicago Bears):** A cuddly and enthusiastic brown bear.
- **Who Dey (Cincinnati Bengals):** A fierce and confident Bengal tiger with bold orange and black stripes.
- **Chomps (Cleveland Browns):** A loyal and spirited brown dog mascot.
- **Rowdy (Dallas Cowboys):** A cheerful and charismatic cowboy with a signature cowboy hat and

boots.

- **Miles (Denver Broncos):** A majestic and proud horse with a strong build, white fur, and an orange mane.
- **Roary (Detroit Lions):** A friendly blue-eyed lion with a gold mane.
- **Toro (Houston Texans):** A strong and resilient blueish bull with an adorable expression.
- **Blue (Indianapolis Colts):** A lively blue horse with a white mane.
- **Jaxson de Ville (Jacksonville Jaguars):** A fun-loving and energetic jaguar with bold spots.
- **K.C. Wolf (Kansas City Chiefs):** A spirited and enthusiastic gray wolf with red and gold team colors.
- **Raider Rusher (Las Vegas Raiders):** A dynamic and agile mascot embodying the fast-paced energy of the Raiders.
- **Rampage (Los Angeles Rams):** A powerful yet cuddly ram with curled horns and a friendly expression.
- **T.D (Miami Dolphins):** A playful and friendly dolphin with a sunny disposition.
- **Viktor (Minnesota Vikings):** A stoic Viking warrior with golden locks and a great beard to boot.
- **Pat Patriot (New England Patriots):** A patriotic and courageous patriot with a tricorn hat.
- **Gumbo and Sir Saint (New Orleans Saints):** Gumbo is a fun-loving dog mascot, while Sir Saint is a noble knight, representing the team's resilience and honor.

- **Swoop (Philadelphia Eagles):** A majestic and proud eagle with a fierce gaze, embodying the soaring spirit of the Eagles.
- **Steely McBeam (Pittsburgh Steelers):** A rugged and determined steelworker with a hard hat and one hell of a jawline.
- **Sourdough Sam (San Francisco 49ers):** A cheerful and friendly gold miner with a cowboy hat and an infectious smile.
- **Blitz and Boom (Seattle Seahawks):** Blitz is a spirited and energetic hawk, while Boom is a powerful and intimidating hawk who, in tandem, captures the thunderous energy of the Seahawks.
- **Captain Fear (Tampa Bay Buccaneers):** A sea-loving and rowdy pirate with a sword.
- **T-Rac (Tennessee Titans):** A fierce, cheeky, and energetic blue-eyed raccoon.
- **Major Tuddy (Washington Commanders):** A patriotic and dignified pig with a military-inspired uniform.

The New York Giants, New York Jets, Los Angeles Chargers, and Green Bay Packers don't have a current mascot, but maybe they'll get one soon to liven up the party!

Afterword

As the clock is about to signal the end of play, we should reflect on the epic journey we have undergone together with our final timeout. This guide has served as a compass for new fans of the sport by thoroughly covering the fundamentals of football. Through our journey, we have unraveled the intricacies of football, which have empowered us to not only understand the action on the field but also to revel in the excitement with every play as passionate fans.

We've covered it all, from player positions and their responsibilities to uncovering the nuances and nature of strategic football plays. Every page of this guide has been designed to help fledgling football fans navigate the exhilarating world of football.

But don't get it twisted—this guide isn't a mere playbook of the rules and formations on a football field but rather a love letter to football itself. We covered the evolution of football going way back to the grassroots of the sport so we could uncover the rich tapestry of football's history, from its humble beginnings to its status as a bedrock of American culture. Along this journey, we learned about iconic players, legendary teams, and game-changing moments that have shaped the course of football history and made it the sport we know and love today.

Yet, that's not all we did. Yes, we learned the fundamentals and the great history of football, but more than that, we explored and embraced the way football has influenced American culture. From tailgating, movies, TV series, video games, fantasy football, and the Super Bowl being an unofficial national holiday, football truly is part of the fabric of American culture. Furthermore, we uncovered pregame traditions for players and teams and unique fan rituals, which further illustrate the camaraderie and passion that define football fandom. Then, of course, we covered the unstoppable plays and game-changing moments in NFL history that will live on in the memories of fans for generations to come.

Football is a sport that truly encapsulates the soul. Take, for instance, my friend. He moved to the USA years ago and was a big cricket and rugby fan, so he never felt the need to give football a try. However, COVID-19 struck, and the world was turned upside down. Being stuck in quarantine, he decided he'd give football a shot, and he instantly fell in love with the sport, even if he was a little confused watching his first few games. He told me he was drawn in by the thrill of the game and the sense of belonging it offered. It wasn't long until he became a super fan, and for the last three or four years, he has been an avid football fanatic. This just goes to show the transformative power of football.

So, team, it's time for our last play. For all of you embarking on your newfound football journey, I am so excited for you, and all I can say is to embrace the passion and camaraderie of football fandom, as it will change your life forever. So, whether you attend a live game, watch at home with friends or family, or join a local fan community, immerse yourself in all the excitement and contagious energy the sport has to offer. This may be the end of our journey together, but always keep the passion for football alive, whether it be through books, documentaries, or podcasts. Stay curious and engaged with your new love for football.

Finally, I want to say thank you to you all for joining me on this journey; it has been a blast! If this guide has enriched your understanding and ignited a passion for football, I'd love to hear from you. Share your thoughts and experiences, and help us continue to inspire future generations of football fans. On three, team: One, two, three, game day!

Glossary

AFC Championship: A championship game in the American Football Conference (AFC), which will determine the AFC's representative at the Super Bowl.

Backfield: The area located behind the line of scrimmage and where each play will begin once the ball is snapped.

Blitz: When the defense sends a higher number of defenders (typically, five or more) to charge the quarterback.

Block: To obstruct defensive players from tackling the ball carrier or sacking the quarterback.

Complete: A successful forward pass from the quarterback that is caught by a receiver.

Down: One of four consecutive attempts for the offense to move the ball at least 10 yards forward.

End zone: Between the goal line and the end line at each end of the field, this is the area where touchdowns are scored.

Field Goal: When a kicker kicks the football in between the football goalposts and above the crossbar for three points.

Gridiron: An alternative to describe an American football field and another name for the sport itself.

Incomplete interception: When a defensive player catches a pass that was intended for an offensive receiver, leading to a turnover.

Line of scrimmage: An imaginary line that stretches the width of the field where the football is placed at the start of a down and on either side of which the offense and defense line up. No player can cross this line before the ball is snapped.

Move the chains: A colloquialism that means the offense is making progress; when the offense achieves a first down, the signal poles on the sidelines (which are essentially 2 tall sticks with a chain connecting them) are moved to the new measurement spot for the next set of four downs.

NFC Championship: A championship game in the National Football Conference (NFC), which will determine the NFC's representative at the Super Bowl.

Overtime: Play that occurs after regular time if the scores are deadlocked after the fourth quarter.

Play: A move or strategic maneuver in a game.

Playoffs: The postseason tournament in which the top teams from each conference compete for the championship title.

Point after: One point is given to a team after their kicker successfully kicks the football between the goalposts and above the crossbar, following a touchdown.

Rush: To gain yardage by running forward with the football.

Sack: A tackle on a quarterback while he possesses the football behind the line of scrimmage.

Scrimmage: The clash of opposing linemen at every down.

Shotgun: When the quarterback lines up for a snap relatively far behind the line of scrimmage.

Snap: When the center passes the ball back from the line of scrimmage to the quarterback and signals the start of each play.

Special Team: Various positions in a football team that are deployed in various game situations, such as kickoffs and attempts at field goals, where the standard offensive and defensive formations are not appropriate.

Super Bowl: The final championship game where the AFC champion will play the NFC champion for the title of the best football team of the season.

Touchdown: The act of catching or running the football in an opponent's end zone.

Wild card games: Playoff games featuring NFL teams that didn't win their respective divisions but still qualified for the postseason due to their impressive regular-season performances.

Bibliography

Allegiant Goods Co. (2022, September 19). *The NFL's 15 best fan traditions, ranked*. Allegiant Goods Co. https://www.allegiantgoods.co/blogs/news/the-nfls-15-best-fan-traditions-ranked

Amber Blog. (2024, March 14). *10 most popular sports in USA you need to keep an eye on*. Amber Student. https://amberstudent.com/blog/post/most-popular-sports-in-usa#:~:text=Also%20known%20as%20grid-iron%2C%20American

American Football International. (2023, June 20). *Introduction to American football strategies*. American Football International. https://www.americanfootballinternational.com/introduction-to-american-football-strategies/

American Management Association. (2020, March 27). *The two-minute drill (TMD): An interview with experts on its use*. Amanet.

Atsbury, M. (2023, August 29). *What is a timeout in American football and how do coaches use them?* DAZN. https://www.dazn.com/en-GB/news/american-football/what-is-a-timeout-in-american-football-and-how-do-coaches-use-them/1nk5k66hml77112jfsif28buzr

Barnwell, B. (2017, July 21). *Barnwell: The NFL stats that matter most*. ESPN.com. https://www.espn.com/nfl/story/_/id/20114211/the-nfl-stats-matter-most-2017-offseason-bill-barnwell

Beasley, B., Greenwald, R., & Agha, N. (2015). NFL time management: The role of timeouts in end-game scenarios. *The Journal of SPORT*, 4(1), 47–64. https://doi.org/10.21038/sprt.2015.0413

Beverly Hills Manners. (2023, October 23). *Manners Monday – Super Bowl etiquette for spectators at the stadium & at home*. Beverly Hills Manners. https://beverlyhillsmanners.com/manners-monday-superbowl-etiquette-for/

Bhandari, L. (2023, June 6). *The influence of American football on popular culture*. NFLGirlUK. https://www.nflgirluk.com/2023/06/06/the-influence-of-american-football-on-popular-culture/

Big Game USA. (2014, November 15). *Why is it Called the Gridiron?* Big

Game USA. https://biggameusa.com/blog/what-does-gridiron-mean.html

Bowen, M. (2018, June 28). *The NFL's most "unstoppable" plays*. Bleacher Report. https://bleacherreport.com/articles/2505575-the-nfls-most-unstoppable-plays

Burd, B. (2023, September 12). *The heart of American football: A brief history of college football*. The Sports Economist. https://thesportsecono mist.com/the-heart-of-american-football-a-brief-history-of-college-football/

By Association. (2017, December 13). *The art of football commentary*. Medium. https://medium.com/@byassociationfc/the-art-of-football-commentary-f69b12d22180

CBS News. (2016, February 4). *Good question: Why is pro football played on Sundays?* CBS Minnesota. https://www.cbsnews.com/minnesota/news/good-question-why-is-pro-football-played-on-sundays/#:~:text=%22Pro%20football%20couldn

Collins Dictionary. (2024, January 15). *Football: Terms used in American football*. Collins Dictionary. Retrieved on 9th May 2024 from, https://www.collinsdictionary.com/word-lists/football-terms-used-in-american-football

Commanders. (2023, April 19). *FedEx Field stadium guide*. https://www.commanders.com/stadium/stadium-guide

Competitive Driving Training. (2018, June 7). *Wide receiver 101 part II: Basics of route running*. GetBetterEveryDay. https://competitivedrive training.wordpress.com/2018/06/07/wide-receiver-101-basics-of-route-running/

Cook, E. (2023, November 27). *How long are timeouts in football?* Playful football https://playfulfootball.com/basics/how-long-are-timeouts-in-football

Dimensions. (2022, February 16). *American football dimensions & drawings*. https://www.dimensions.com/element/american-football

Dix, B. (2023, February 1). *A compilation of Tom Brady's career stats and accolades*. Buccaneers. https://www.buccaneers.com/news/tom-brady-career-stats-records-nfl-2000-2022-patriots-bucs

Dockett, E. (2024, January 10). *NFL football penalties explained*. HowThey-Play. https://howtheyplay.com/team-sports/Football-Penalties-Explained#:~:text=Players%20are%20only%20ejected%20if

Ducksters. (2019a). *Football: How to tackle.* https://www.ducksters.com/sports/football/how_to_tackle.php

Ducksters. (2019b, June 16). *Football: Strategy and tactics.* https://www.ducksters.com/sports/footballstrategy.php

Ducksters. (2020). *Football: Offense basics.* https://www.ducksters.com/sports/football/offense_basics.php

Ducksters. (2022a, July 16). *Football: Defense basics.* https://www.ducksters.com/sports/football/defense_basics.php

Ducksters. (2022b, August 27). *Football: Officials and refs.* https://www.ducksters.com/sports/football/officials_referees.php

Ducksters. (2022c, September 22). *Football: Offensive formations.* https://www.ducksters.com/sports/football/offensive_formations.php

Ducksters. (2023, July 9). *Football: Defensive formations.* https://www.ducksters.com/sports/football/defensive_formations.php

Dummies. (2016, March 26). *The American football player's uniform.* Dummies. https://www.dummies.com/article/home-auto-hobbies/sports-recreation/fantasy-sports/fantasy-football/the-american-football-players-uniform-186809/

Fadullon, J. (2022, September 7). *Updating and ranking the 50 greatest NFL players of all-time.* ClutchPoints. https://clutchpoints.com/updating-and-ranking-the-50-greatest-nfl-players-of-all-time

Fleming, F. (2023, October 25). *Key NFL stats that matter most.* SportingPost. https://www.sportingpost.com/sports-betting/most-important-stats-in-football/

Focus Gaming News. (2023, June 21). *How long does an NFL game last? + other useful things to know.* https://focusgn.com/how-long-does-an-nfl-game-last

Football Coach Insider. (2023, March 1). *Identifying and correcting risky tackle technique in American football.* Coaches Insider. https://coachesinsider.com/football/identifying-and-correcting-risky-tackle-technique-in-american-football/

Football Toolbox. (2017, February 2). *Short yardage and goal line defense.* Football Toolbox. https://footballtoolbox.net/short-yardage-and-goal-line-defense

Ford Field. (2023, February 12). *Prohibited items during NFL events.* Ford Field. https://www.fordfield.com/assets/doc/Prohibited-Items-NFL-Events-a3e72c4ea6.pdf

FOX Sport. (2024, February 12). *What are the new NFL overtime playoff rules? Everything you need to know.* https://www.foxsports.com/stories/nfl/what-to-know-about-the-new-nfl-overtime-rules-ahead-of-the-playoffs

Fox Sports. (2024, March 22). *2023 NFL leaders & stats - team rushing stats.* https://www.foxsports.com/nfl/team-stats?category=rushing&season=2023

Gamble, A. (2024, January 19). *Taylor Swift binge-watches Netflix to learn about NFL and impress Travis Kelce.* The Mirror. https://www.mirror.co.uk/sport/other-sports/american-sports/nfl-netflix-swift-kelce-chiefs-31924247

Gosling, R. (2022, September 15). *List of NFL mascots.* Pro Football Network. https://www.profootballnetwork.com/list-of-nfl-mascots/

Gridiron Sport. (2023, September 19). *The top 14 best NFL fan traditions ranked.* https://thegridironsport.com/the-top-14-best-nfl-fan-traditions-ranked/

Griffiths, A. (2023, September 4). *American football & NFL positions explained. Roles in football.* Net World Sports Blog. https://blog.networldsports.co.uk/american-football-positions-explained/

Haddad, C. (2024a, February 12). *How many players on a football team? Learn the players - vIQtory sports.* VIQtory. https://www.viqtorysports.com/in-american-football-how-many-players-are-on-the-field/#:~:text=NFL%20Team%20roster%20only%20allows

Haddad, C. (2024b, February 12). *The complete beginners guide to American football.* VIQtory Sports. https://www.viqtorysports.com/how-to-understand-american-football-beginners-guide/

Hawkins, J. (2023, March 19). *American football around the world: Uncovering the global impact of the sport.* American Football To. https://www.americanfootballtoday.com/post/american-football-around-the-world-uncovering-the-global-impact-of-the-sport#:~:text=American%20football%20has%20made%20a

Hillyer, B. (2022, October 18). *A brief history of American football: From its origins to the present day.* The Atmore Advance. https://www.atmoreadvance.com/2022/10/18/a-brief-history-of-american-football-from-its-origins-to-the-present-day/

Hoffman, R. (2011, June 28). *NFL rankings: The 16 best NFL rule changes in history.* Bleacher Report. https://bleacherreport.com/articles/748241-nfl-rankings-the-16-best-nfl-rule-changes-in-history

Holder, L. (2023, May 25). *NFL kickoff variations through the years and how it compares to other leagues*. The Athletic. https://theathletic.com/4552820/2023/05/25/nfl-kickoff-rules-changes/

Hutchison, C. (2016, September 19). *The 7 most common defenses in football*. ACTIVEkids. https://www.activekids.com/football/articles/the-7-most-common-defenses-in-football/slide-7

Jansen, O. (2022, February 18). *Gang tackle*. Sports Definitions. https://www.sportsdefinitions.com/american-football/gang-tackle/

Joseph, S. (2024, March 27). *The way NFL games start is drastically changing after team owners approve new kickoff rule*. CNN. https://edition.cnn.com/2024/03/27/sport/nfl-kickoff-rule-changes-2024-spt-intl/index.html

Keep the score. (2024, February 9). *How does football scoring work?* https://keepthescore.com/blog/posts/football-scoring/

Ki, R. (2023, December 16). *The NFL's impact on American culture: A look at football's role in society*. Footballr.news. https://www.footballr.news/football/the-nfls-impact-on-american-culture-a-look-at-footballs-role-in-society/

Kuch, M. (2024, January 24). *American football history: Timeline & how it started*. Sports Foundation. https://sportsfoundation.org/american-football-history/

Long, H., & Czarnecki, J. (2017, April 24). *List of football penalties (NFL)*. Dummies. https://www.dummies.com/article/home-auto-hobbies/sports-recreation/fantasy-sports/fantasy-football/common-penalties-in-american-football-187974/

Manfull, L. (2013, August 14). *Fundamental principles of offensive blocking*. Coaches Insider. https://coachesinsider.com/football/fundamental-principles-of-offensive-blocking/

Martin, C. (2022, January 12). *Shotgun formation offense (coaching guide with images)*. Football Advantage. https://footballadvantage.com/shotgun-formation/

McCarriston, S. (2024, February 13). *Every Super Bowl halftime performer in history: Usher, Rihanna, Eminem, Prince, Michael Jackson and more*. CBSSports.com. https://www.cbssports.com/nfl/news/every-super-bowl-halftime-performer-in-history-usher-rihanna-eminem-prince-michael-jackson-and-more/

Millennial Football. (2021, April 18). *Millennial football - run blocking techniques*. Sam Fleener. https://www.samfleener.com/football/offense-fundamentals/offensive-line/run-blocking-techniques

Molski, M. (2023, May 4). *Everything to know about NFL schedule, how it works*. NBC Sports Chicago. https://www.nbcsportschicago.com/nfl/ chicago-bears/everything-to-know-about-nfl-schedule-how-it-works/ 324619/

New England Patriots. (2006, March 30). *Red Hickey, shotgun formation inventor, dies.* https://www.patriots.com/news/red-hickey-shotgun-formation-inventor-dies-168491

NFL. (2019, September 20). *NFL's 100 greatest plays: The final five unveiled*. NFL. https://www.nfl.com/news/nfl-s-100-greatest-plays-the-final-five-unveiled-0ap3000001056879

NFL. (2022a, November 15). *NFL 100*. NFL. https://www.nfl.com/100/ originals/100-greatest/plays-4

NFL. (2022b). *The 60-minutes medical meeting*. NFL. https://www.nfl. com/playerhealthandsafety/health-and-wellness/player-care/the-60-minutes-meeting-a-critical-game-day-checkpoint

NFL. (2023). *The NFL international series | NFL football operations*. NDL. https://operations.nfl.com/journey-to-the-nfl/the-nfl-s-international-impact/the-nfl-international-series/

NFL. (2024, March 13). *NFL.com | official site of the National Football League*. NFL. https://www.nfl.com/stats/team-stats/offense/passing/ 2023/reg/all

NFL Flag. (2024, January 20). *How to catch a football*. NFL Flag. https:// nflflag.com/coaches/football-drills/how-to-catch-a-football#:~:text=For%20example%2C%20if%20a%20pass

NFL Football Operations. (2022a, September 17). *Chop block*. Operations NFL. https://operations.nfl.com/the-rules/nfl-video-rulebook/chop-block/

NFL Football Operations. (2022b, December 6). *Illegal block above the waist*. Operations NFL. https://operations.nfl.com/the-rules/nfl-video-rulebook/illegal-block-above-the-waist/#:~:text=Penalty%3A%20-For%20an%20illegal%20block

NFL Football Operations. (2023, March 8). *The NFL competition committee*. Operations NFL. https://operations.nfl.com/the-rules/the-nfl-competition-committee/#:~:text=The%20NFL

NFL Football Operations. (2024a, February 17). *Countdown to kickoff: How NFL games happen*. Operations NFL. https://operations.nfl.com/game day/pre-game/countdown-to-kickoff/

NFL Football Operations. (2024b, February 20). *NFL jersey numbers*. Operations NFL. https://operations.nfl.com/the-rules/rules-changes/nfl-jersey-numbers/

Oliver, E. (2024, February 12). *Who has kicked the longest field goal in NFL history?* The Analyst. https://theanalyst.com/eu/2024/02/longest-field-goal-in-nfl-history/

Pistone, A. (2022, April 12). *Ranking the 5 most successful teams in NFL history.* Sportskeeda. https://www.sportskeeda.com/nfl/the-5-most-successful-teams-nfl-history

Pitman, K. (2024, January 29). *Can you believe Patrick Mahomes has broken all these records?* Lonestar 99.5. https://lonestar995fm.com/can-you-believe-patrick-mahomes-has-broken-all-these-records/

Pro Football Hall of Fame. (2017a). *Lawrence Taylor.* Pro Football Hall of Fame. https://www.profootballhof.com/players/lawrence-taylor/

Pro Football Hall of Fame. (2017b, May 8). *Joe Montana.* Pro Football Hall of Fame. https://www.profootballhof.com/players/joe-montana/

Pro Football Hall of Fame. (2018, September 11). *Jim Brown.* Pro Football Hall of Fame.. https://www.profootballhof.com/players/jim-brown/

Raiders. (2024, January 19). *Las Vegas Raiders.* Las Vegas Raiders. https://www.raiders.com/history/jerry-rice#:~:text=Owner%20of%2038%20NFL%20career

Richmond, S. (2023, November 6). *1st college football game ever was New Jersey vs. Rutgers in 1869.* NCAA. https://www.ncaa.com/news/football/article/2017-11-06/college-football-history-heres-when-1st-game-was-played#:~:text=Rutgers%20and%20New%20Jersey%20(later

Riddle, R. (2012, August 8). *What NFL pros do in the hours just before a game.* Bleacher Report. https://bleacherreport.com/articles/1289216-what-the-pros-do-in-the-hours-just-before-a-game

Riddle, R. (2013, October 3). *What really goes on in an NFL locker room at halftime?* Bleacher Report. https://bleacherreport.com/articles/1796628-what-really-goes-on-in-an-nfl-locker-room-at-halftime

Rolfe, B. (2021, September 12). *How long is a football game? Breaking down the time between the first and last whistle.* Pro Football Network. https://www.profootballnetwork.com/how-long-is-a-football-game-breaking-down-the-time-between-the-first-and-last-whistle/

Rookie Road. (2022a, November 14). *Football angle tackle.* https://www.rookieroad.com/football/skills-and-techniques/angle-tackle/

Rookie Road. (2022b, November 16). *Football blocking.* https://www.rookieroad.com/football/skills-and-techniques/blocking/

Rookie Road. (2023a, May 30). *Football penalty list.* https://www.rookieroad.com/football/penalties/

Rookie Road. (2023b, July 10). *What counts as A tackle in football?* https://www.rookieroad.com/football/questions/what-counts-as-a-tackle/

Rookie Road. (2023c, July 12). *Football coin toss.* https://www.rookieroad.com/football/101/coin-toss/

Rookie Road. (2023d, October 13). *Football kickoff.* https://www.rookieroad.com/football/kick-types/kickoff/

Rookie Road. (2024, January 31). *Football special teams.* https://www.rookieroad.com/football/101/special-teams/

Rules of Sport. (2019). *American football rules.* Rules of Sport.com. https://www.rulesofsport.com/sports/american-football.html

Ryan, B. (2022, October 8). *Understanding what is clipping in football.* My Football News. https://myfootballnews.com/what-is-clipping-in-football/

Schuller, R. (2024, February 13). *Which NFL team has the most Super Bowl wins?* DAZN. https://www.dazn.com/en-GB/news/american-football/which-nfl-team-has-the-most-super-bowl-wins/484faigcpnwi1foytqsaoagq3

Spajic, D. J. (2022a, June 2). *Origin of American football: From ancient Rome to Super Bowl.* Play Today. https://playtoday.co/blog/stats/origin-of-american-football/

Spajic, D. J. (2022b, September 30). *20 NFL facts & stats: Unforgettable football moments.* Play Today. https://playtoday.co/blog/stats/nfl-facts/

Sportskeeda. (2024). *Travis Kelce.* Sportskeeda. https://www.sportskeeda.com/nfl/travis-kelce#travis-kelce-14

StatMuse. (2024, February 10). *Team average solo tackles per game.* StatMuse. https://www.statmuse.com/nfl/ask/team-average-solo-tackles-per-game

Sutton, B. (2019, February 25). *Offensive line technique 101, part 2: Hand placement.* The Phinsider. https://www.thephinsider.com/2019/2/25/18236553/offensive-line-technique-101-part-hand-placement-miami-dolphins-trenches-play-leverage-guard-tackle

Tallent, A. (2023, February 2). *Tom Brady: 5 records that will never be broken.* AthlonSports.com. https://athlonsports.com/nfl/tom-brady-records-that-will-never-be-broken

Team Color Codes. (2022, April 18). *NFL team color codes hex, RGB,*

PANTONE and CMYK. Team Color Codes. https://teamcolorcodes. com/nfl-team-color-codes/

The Big Lead. (2023, May 23). *How many games are in the NFL season?* The Big Lead. https://www.thebiglead.com/posts/how-many-games-in-nfl-season-01h14gb26qwj

The Denver Post. (2023, April 8). *Peyton Manning's NFL records*. The Denver Post. https://extras.denverpost.com/charts/broncos/peyton-manning-records/

The Wander Club. (2022, September 19). *15 interesting NFL facts you probably didn't know*. The Wander Club. https://thewanderclub.com/blogs/blog/interesting-nfl-facts-you-probably-didnt-know

Touchdown Tips. (2016, June 4). *So what's this tailgating thing anyway?* Touchdown Trips. https://touchdowntrips.com/2016/06/04/whats-tailgating/

Turf Tank. (2022, November 7). *How big is a football field?* Turf Tank. https://turftank.com/us/academy/how-big-is-a-football-field/

Tutorials point. (2024, February 9). *American football*. Tutorials Point. https://www.tutorialspoint.com/american_football/american_football_quick_guide.htm

University Living. (2023, December 18). *Top and most popular sports in USA*. University News and Updates. https://www.universityliving.com/blog/beyond-uni/most-popular-sports-in-usa/#:~:text=It%20is%20the%20biggest%20sport

Vault, T. (2023, November 14). *Types of American football special teams plays*. Tagvault.org. https://tagvault.org/blog/types-of-american-football-special-teams-plays/

Vult, D. (2015, December 1). *Unwritten rules: To stand or to sit at the stadium*. Cincy Jungle. https://www.cincyjungle.com/2015/12/1/9829336/bengals-stadium-etiquette-to-stand-or-to-sit-that-is-the-question

Wilmesherr, K. (2022, July 10). *American football monthly - zone blocking, part II – footwork and blocking scheme*. American Football Monthly. https://www.americanfootballmonthly.com/Subaccess/articles.php?article_id=6004&output=article#:~:text=When%20executing%20the%20footwork%20for

Youth Football Online. (2016, July 26). *Open field tackling techniques*. Youth Football Online. https://youthfootballonline.com/open-field-tackling-techniques-insert-more-keywords/

Youth Football Online. (2023, September 5). *Understanding and coaching wide receiver route stems*. Youth Football Online. https://youthfootbal lonline.com/understanding-and-coaching-wide-receiver-route-stems/ #google_vignette

IMAGE REFERENCES

Buscema, J. (2021). *The player scores a touchdown* [Image]. Unsplash. https://unsplash.com/photos/football-players-on-field-during-daytime-8XeZNEKgm-w

Curiel, A. (2017). *NFL wall* [Image]. Unsplash. https://unsplash.com/ photos/nfl-logo-KgYazRO3l8A

Goldsberry, P. (2019). *Fans watching football at home* [Image]. Unsplash. https://unsplash.com/photos/person-in-blue-nba-dallas-mavericks-crew-neck-shirt-sitting-while-holding-bowl-with-potato-chips-Ldl5WoUQmBk

Johnston, K. (2017a). *A football player is running with the ball* [Image]. Unsplash. https://unsplash.com/photos/two-nfl-players-on-green-grass-UjCvO-LzKpM

Johnston, K. (2017b). *Football players battle for position in a college football game* [Image]. Unsplash. https://unsplash.com/photos/two-nfl-players-ym7zKXHdCSY

Johnston, K. (2019). Football catch [Image]. Pixabay. https://pixabay.com/ photos/football-american-football-player-1490180/

Johnstone, K. (2017). *A college football player prepares to begin a game with a kickoff.* [Image]. Unsplash. https://unsplash.com/photos/three-football-players-running-towards-football-ball-at-field-during-daytime-ZH66-9B04cw

Keithjj. (2022a). *Football tackle* [Image]. Pixabay. https://pixabay.com/ photos/football-american-football-ball-1518040/

Keithjj. (2022b). *Football team chatting amongst each other* [Image]. Pixabay. https://pixabay.com/photos/american-football-football-team-team-1465510/

Keithjj. (2024a). *American football fan with face painted* [Image]. Pixabay. https://pixabay.com/photos/american-football-fan-supporter-1505842/

Keithjj. (2024b). *American football officials* [Image]. Pixabay. https:// pixabay.com/photos/american-football-1464551/

Keithjj. (2024c). *Quarterback throwing a forward pass* [Image]. Pixabay.

https://pixabay.com/photos/football-american-football-players-1485698/

Keithjj. (2024d). *Sack* [Image]. Pixabay. https://pixabay.com/photos/football-american-football-game-1501696/

Keithjj. (2024e). *Texans quarterback* [Image]. Pixabay. https://pixabay.com/photos/quarterback-american-football-action-1579458/

Li, Z. (2024). *Football field* [Image]. Pixabay. https://www.pexels.com/photo/healthy-light-city-field-13811359/

Library of Congress. (2019). *Early days of American Football* [Image]. Unsplash. https://unsplash.com/photos/football-players-red-grange-and-joe-zeller-during-practice-nJD0PWqDOBw

mauricioglucas. (2024). *Barbecue in the street* [Image]. Pixabay. https://pixabay.com/photos/barbecue-in-the-street-beef-barbecue-4281088/

Pixabay. (2023). *Football center getting ready to snap the ball* [Image]. Pexels. https://www.pexels.com/photo/football-player-game-position-163398/

Pixabay. (2024). *Football assisted tackle* [Image]. Pixabay. https://pixabay.com/photos/football-american-players-teams-90894/

Unsplash+. (2022). *Timeout* [Image]. Unsplash. https://unsplash.com/photos/a-group-of-football-players-kneel-down-on-the-field-NvANG2wuKPo

Verduzco, M. (2023). *Playbook on a football field* [Image]. Unsplash. https://unsplash.com/photos/a-notebook-sitting-on-the-side-of-a-football-field-Rn6n5Lh1BdA

Williams, J. (2021). *American football* [Image]. Unsplash. https://unsplash.com/photos/a-close-up-of-a-football-on-a